Vibrationa

Readings

A Sacred Geometry of the Self

**GOLDEN POINT
CRESTONE, COLORADO**

Vibrational Healing Cards

Readings

A Sacred Geometry of the Self

Rowena Pattee Kryder

GOLDEN POINT
CRESTONE, COLORADO

library of congress catalog number: 97-93104
ISBN   0-9624716-5-8

Golden Point Productions
PO BOX 685
Crestone, CO 81131

www.creative-harmonics.org

Text, symbols, illustrations and cover design by Rowena Pattee Kryder, Ph.D.

Printed in Hong Kong through Pacific Rim International.

Contents

Introduction..1

Readings, Visualizations, and Affirmations...........8

Medicine Path Introduction and Charts...........136

Old Earth Path Readings....................................145

New Earth Path Readings....................................158

Planes between Old Earth and New Earth......171

This work is dedicated to the One Ever-abiding Consciousness present in every being, not the least of which are mentioned below:

grasses, bugs,
bees, birds, insects, stars,
moons, worms, seasons, trees, flys,
stones, oceans, mountains, fire, air, water,
earth, elemental spirits, atoms, molecules, cells. Danny
Abel, Crystal Adams, Roe Adams, Robert Aiken, Omram
Mikael Aivanov, Joel and Serafina Andrews, Joe Campbell,
Joyce Cochran, Cathy Colman, Dominie Cappadonna,
Sister Mirium Clare, Dale Clark, Flora Courtois, Roger
Davis, Howard Dugan, Sanje Elliott, Wally and Julianne
Everett, Aroshyn Gebrandzen, Irina Harford, John Haugse,
Ruth-Inge Heinze, Shanja Kirstann, Eleanor Kryder,Mark
& Sandy Kryder, Dick and Karen Kryder, Charlie Leary,
Roger & Jeanne Long, Richard Lucas, Ana Holub, Anne &
Hank Maiden, Randy Masters, Avon Mattison, Ralph
Metzner, Anita Rui Olds, Laurence Ostrow, Sister Palmo,
Vaughn Perret, Barbara Pettee, Rocco, Alma Rose, Will &
Kalima Sawyer, Sylvia & Lawrence Schechter, Rupert
Sheldrake, Mark & Karen Sullivan, Shunyata, Shunryu
Suzuki Roshi, Tat, Diana Vandenberg, Jack Wilkinson,
MilesWilkinson, Joy & Leonard Williamson, Howard Wills,
Acrissa Laughing Wolf, Fred Alan Wolf, Jack & Patty
Wright, Devas, Angels, Archangels, Goddesses, Gods,
spirits, star-beings, ghosts, demons,
Ascended Masters, Divine
Councils, God

and many others. . . all wholes within the One Love-Light

Introduction

The *Vibrational Healing Cards* contain a comprehensive set of sixty-four vibrational seed-forms that, when brought into consciousness, can enhance our chakras and energetically purify and heal our subtle vehicles.

We are all dis-eased in so far as we identify with being a separate self. "I" is a word that divides from the "other", initiating a split into polarities that become more and more complex the more we get attached to one side of any pair of opposites: inner and outer, good and evil, me and you, true and false etc. All of these polarities create a vibrating tension like a musical string that "hums" whenever our consciousness strikes it. The tensions of opposites actually create an unconscious "hum" of vibrations through our physical bodies and subtle bodies (etheric, astral, mental, spiritual) that is in the background of our lives all the time. It is these vibrating tensions—conscious or unconscious—that we experience as joy, sorrow, peace and conflicts, health and disease.

The divine Word is vibration. The law of vibration or harmony governs the influences upon soul and body in this world. On the most concrete level, the vibrational laws of sound, electromagnetism, gravity and sub-atomic physics are descriptions of how the universal law of vibration manifests in the physical world.

The laws of vibration work on higher, more subtle planes of being through diverse states of consciousness. Vibrations work through patterns. Everything in this world vibrates. The power of thought is a powerful vibration. And soul manifests in gradations of refinement of vibrations. Our true Self is not the body, yet vibrations harmonize or disharmonize the body as a temporary vehicle for practise in finding the essence of our being.

Disease results from disharmony of our various vehicles and/or of one part or organ in relation to the whole. Images, thoughts, and feelings are ways that beliefs are stored and expressed. Suppressed images, thoughts, and feelings need to emerge in order to be erased or uprooted. These suppressed patterns have karma at the root of them. Karma (we reap what we sow) is also under the laws of vibration. Karma can be transmuted and cleared by changing vibrations.

The Unity of the Love-Light

Any healing effect you may experience using these cards depends on your consciousness becoming one with the core vibration of a given card and passing into the One Source, the Love-Light from whence all healing comes. This is not to say the card does the healing, but that a card is a pattern that may provide a porthole to the One Source that heals. This One Source is undefinable, eternal, without limits and is Unity Itself.

To express the Primordial Unity in words is actually impossible! Yet, as Chuang Tsu said, "Words are not just blown air. They have a meaning . . . Words seem different from the chirping of birds." He continues by saying, "At first Tao had no name. Words are not eternal. Because of words there are distinctions."* In Chuang Tzu's time and culture "Tao" was used as a word to point beyond words, in much the same way I use the words Unity, One Source and Love-Light.

As human beings with bodies, psyches, minds and spirits, we grow up in conditioned families and cultures that limit our capacity to receive primordial unity. Conditioning leads us to make discernments, value-judgements and choices. This necessary vibrational conflict and buildup of tension is part of our time-space experience. But once having tasted of the dual state, it is possible to be aware of this condition and let it go, releasing attachment to both sides of the polarity and be healed.

I call the primordial Unity, the Love-Light. It is undivided, eternal and is completely inherent in all phenomena of the universe. The Love-Light is in our bodies. We are fundamentally made of Love-Light.

This Love-Light embraces the polarity of light and darkness, love and hate, and all other polarities. From our conditioned vantage of polarity, the Love-Light appears as nothing, voidness. The vibrational tensions that compose our subtle and physical bodies cease in this void that is also the Love-Light. We become relaxed awareness when the tensions of polarities are released.

That which I call the Love-Light is a direct experience. The Love-Light is experienced when our consciousness—our being—reveals itself as beyond, yet inclusive of, duality. Life experiences guide us to this state of Grace. Sometimes it is by "hard knocks"—illness, death of a beloved, attacks, business losses—that the intensity of our attention is caught in enough suffering to change our consciousness. We may then raise our awareness to the nondual state of consciousness and receive the Love-Light. Or we may choose consciously to be receptive to the divine source—the primordial Unity. The reception of the Love-Light is itself divine Grace and the beginning of holistic healing.

Our healing is likely experienced to take place in layers over a period of time, though its source—the Love-Light—is without limits of time or space. As the vibrational tensions are relaxed—from the causal level through the mental, astral, etheric and physical—the polarity of our desires and fears is released; and all with which we previously identified becomes void. Healing, in other words, may be experienced as disorientation—for our familiar tensions are relaxed and our tendency toward grasping and attachment-as-identity vanishes.

Each of the sixty-four *Vibrational Healing Cards* has a unique pattern of vibration. As a whole, the cards span from the highest spiritual vibration through the psyche, body and mind and the four realms of nature, including specific social-cultural vibrations. Each card is specific to a given quality—like a melody or series of chords—in our field of experiences, and yet holds tension in balance and harmony. This harmonization of qualities makes possible a release of our conditioned, chronic and reactive, acute tensions when we meditate on their colors and forms. The words of the text for each card assist in opening us to the Love-Light and yet give us awareness of more relative practises and suggestions as well. In other words, the cards and their readings are vibrational mediators between our vibrational tensions—our conflicts and diseases—and the Love-Light, the One Source.

In the primordial Unity of the Love-Light there is no experience but there is pure *Being*. Yet without the polarity of self and other, subject and object, knower and known, we would not have this experience of tension and strife, passion and terror, and all that makes up what we ordinarily know as life. But when we tire of strife, disease, confusion or even boredom and apathy, it is time to cease wanting to know or to do, to achieve, or progress, and just BE.

Old Earth and New Earth Complementarity of Each Card

There is a complementarity within each card, but not a polarity: This complementarity is revealed in the Old Earth and New Earth qualities which are upside down to each other as words and symbols on the ends of each card. These words do not indicate an opposite to each other, but a heightening towards the Love-Light in the New Earth. Old Earth is not bad and something to overcome, but simply a reflection in the mirror of consciousness that may be happening at any given moment, based on past cultures and personal conditioning.

For example, you may be having an intense experience and if you pick the intensity card, it calls your attention to the fact and gives you a spiral passage to its release. Meditating on the card and its meaning, you may relax your intense effort to make it happen, get involved, or play out a passion. Then you—the subject—become free of the object that brought on the intensity and instead of self-centered, you become open to the energy that is flowing through you as the Love-Light. Then the intensity changes to wholeheartedness—which is not attached to a result or object and is vibrationally harmonious to what is actually happening. The energy of your being can respond and become one

4

with the Love-Light in some daily life situation where you can be wholehearted.

If you picked this card so that wholeheartedness was the orientation of the card in the first place, then you can meditate on the card as a color and form vibration that reflects your open and all-embracing state. You may become one with the Love-Light as your awareness becomes more and more clear. From this state you can also embrace intensity and have compassion for yourself and others who are being intense. There is no need to judge intensity as something inferior or to be overcome. From the Love-Light of wholeheartedness you can empathize with intensity without getting involved or hooked on its qualities of self-centered energy. Wholeheartedness contains intensity; whereas intensity can transform into wholeheartedness. The New Earth qualities are instantaneous—opening to the Old Earth; whereas the Old Earth qualities take time and space to transform into the New Earth qualities.

Procedure

After shuffling the cards and cutting three times, either pick one off the top or spread them out in front of you and pick one. Notice which number and word faces you (right side up). That is the one that is most actively relevant. Look up the reading. The best way to find the reading is to look at the side of the card which is Old Earth (the lower number of the two) and find the reading in this book. The Old Earth runs forward in sequence from 1 to 65 while the New Earth counterparts run in sequence (from the front of the book toward the back) in reverse—from 128 to 65.

The basic reading is a thought-feeling complex. If you can, have someone read it to you as you meditate on the card. Meditate on the form and colors of the card. These are vibrational patterns that can harmonize various levels of your being. Read the visualization. Again, if possible, have someone read it to you while you are in a meditative state. Let the visualizations become a transformation of thought and feeling. Say the affirmation aloud. Repeat it to yourself throughout the day, before you go to sleep at night and when you awake. The affirmations keep our consciousness in resonance with the divine Spirit.

The "seed-pattern" of each card can be imagined extruding into a wavefield of its unique geometry. You might draw this wavefield and then meditate within it—visualizing its form around you, vibrating. Then you can color in the pattern while feeling its energy.

Each and every card can be a door to your Self, meeting the divine Spirit and resonating together. We can enter into Spirit to the degree we are free of dissonant negations—(born of negative thought-forms and feelings, which become beliefs). We need to reduce our thought-forms to the essentials and liberate our cellular memory from old traumas of suppression, rage, confusion and illusion.

The subconscious is our inner child, and this child needs to be free of erroneous baggage of wounded thought-forms if we are to be whole. To meditate deeply on the forms of the *Vibrational Medicine Cards* is to enter into a field of vibrations which can clear the subconscious if we are devoted enough—to our unconditional Truth.

There may be a resistance at first to certain cards. If we strongly like or dislike some form, we are likely not in balance and harmony with our conscious and subconscious minds in that area. The super-conscious or Spirit takes care of itself. Its presence comes in as the Love-Light when we release the unessential.

Liberation from suffering is easier than our habit-patterns and unconscious beliefs "think" it to be. Let us open our consciousness to receive healing on all levels; let us have confidence. The "future" will not be like the "past." We can choose, each moment, how to live our lives. Let us trust the process. The affirmations work on our subconscious minds and can deliver us from millenia of illusions. Let us trust ourselves. Enjoy the *Vibrational Healing Cards* and be happy!

1 Eternity

Your true nature is eternal, incorruptible, with neither beginning nor end. Rest your awareness in the truth of your eternal being, which is free in unutterable simplicity. Let go of all worry, attachments, or thoughts. Allow the spontaneous, boundless and timeless nature of eternity to sweep aside and dissolve all feelings or thoughts of limitation, of gain or loss. Make no war on distractions, thoughts, or any beings—for there is nothing that can obscure the eternal presence of undivided consciousness. Find a quiet place and be still. With silent ease open your awareness to what is and eternity will be your friend.

BE STILL

Visualize and feel Eternity focussed in your heart, then flooding your whole being. Eternity says, "Be still. Change any reactive energy to stillness. Breathing naturally, regularly, just be aware of the stillness of your being. Know this as the incorruptible source."

Affirmation:
Each instant, I feel and intuitively know eternity within me.

128 Compassion

Dear beloved. As you fully realize your oneness with all sentient beings, your heart will open to the sick, the hurt, the helpless, and the dying. This is a great art and mystery of transforming poison into medicine. Fear not pollution or being hurt by others, for as you include and embrace even your "enemies" the stream of conflict and suffering in your own being will cease. Compassion cannot be contained or limited, yet it embraces all. Negativity and its roots are burned like incense in fire and dissolved like salt in water when the generous flow of compassion floods your being. Respond to people and situations around you with gentle kindness. You are love in blessed companionship with all and any who are near or far.

CARE FOR YOURSELF

Visualize and feel Compassion as a golden elixir created in your own heart. Compassion says, "Love the ugly, the sick, and the difficult as much as the beautiful, the healthy, and the easy. Transmute the of poison the world and it will turn to medicine in the crucible of your heart."

Affirmation:

I care for and respond compassionately to every situation as it arises.

2 *Divine Eye*

Your clear awareness remains in boundlessness as you perceive each person, place, and event with equanimity. Focus without attachment or judgement and let things be as they are. Witness what is happening within and without. Free yourself of desire or hatred for anything. Your likes and dislikes make no difference now. Just look and see how it is. Reactions will disappear when you let go of specific results. Be in the flow of naked awareness, letting your gaze be open, wide and at peace with how things are. Nothing can ever be changed without first seeing it as it is. Be simply aware, moment by moment, and you will realize all is well.

BE OPEN WHILE FOCUSSED

Visualize and feel the Divine Eye in your third eye in the center of your forehead. Divine Eye says, "Concentrate and dilate. Change distractions to single-pointed concentration. Change contraction to openness. What do you see possible in this perspective?"

Affirmation:
With open heart and mind, I see how things are.

127 Everywhere

Your vision can be as vast as space when you cease concentrating, thinking, and grasping. Let your gaze be unfocused, diffused, and open to the unknown and the apparently invisible. Look *around* people rather than *at* them. Behold the mystery of their energy at one with the ground of consciousness that you share with them. The Love-Light is everywhere. To behold it is to allow the Love-Light to shine through your being so that you see others with unconditional love. Space is everywhere. Realize the indivisibility of space within each creature, plant, and person. The limitless simplicity of space within your own being will radiate the clear Light everywhere.

BEHOLD THE LOVE-LIGHT EVERYWHERE

Visualize and feel Everywhere as the branches of a great tree,
spreading throughout the world, filled with flowers and fruits.
Everywhere says, "Cease giving your power away. The divine
elixir will spread to the farthest reaches of your world. Extend
to others the abundance that comes to you
and feel your link with beings."

Affirmation:
*I see the mystery in and around people and events through a spacious
acceptance.*

3 Spiritual Fire

Your focus can now energize you to feel the spiritual fire emanate from your chakras (subtle energy centers). Allow your attention to enter these subtle energy areas of your subtle body as you breathe naturally, quietly, and consciously. Be aware that all is Light in diverse frequencies and intensities—the trees, creatures, and your very body. If you feel disturbed by anything whatsoever, meditation on this card and feeling the vibrations of Love-Light within your own being will synchronize the inner and outer, dispelling any disharmonious wavelengths. The spiritual fire purifies and harmonizes your subtle bodies, bringing both a sense of purpose and peace.

RADIATE FROM WITHIN

Visualize and feel Spiritual Fire radiating from your whole being. Spiritual Fire says, "Radiate from within. Change passivity to radiant, creative energy. Energize and activate your whole being from within."

Affirmation:
*I feel Spiritual Fire in every fibre of my being
and can harmoniously energize any aspect of myself.*

126 Luminosity

All your strenuous seeking and effort can be released while the Love-Light in your being floods into an incandescence. Let go of all drama—of being a victim or a conqueror, and be aware that everything—cells, flowers, stones, as well as stars—are luminous Love-Light. Your very being is luminosity. Let the bliss of selflessness shine through and your way will be lit clearly and instantly, moment by moment. Cease seeking answers and courageously trust the wise, open Love-Light. Breathe in luminosity and you will breathe out luminosity as well. Dark thoughts and feelings vanish when the luminosity of being shines. Cease clinging to self-righteous ideas and values and allow yourself to become transparent to the Love-Light.

BREATHE THE LOVE-LIGHT

Visualize and feel Luminosity as the vivification of the radiant consciousness within you. Luminosity says, "Embrace the dark, the heavy, the evil and it will be made light through my self-luminous power. When you are luminous within you have no fear of darkness. How will you go about maintaining your light?"

Affirmation:
My whole being is luminous with Love-Light which clearly guides me.

4 Crown of Light

Now you can shine with inexhaustible Love-Light. Give up all ambivalence and surrender to the Light that permeates your being and all worlds. This nondual state is essential to realizing when you are confused, attracted, or repelled by one thing or another. You create any conflicts you may have with a clinging consciousness. Let the Light shine through your crown and all through your being. There is nothing that is not of the Love-Light. The divine aura is vast and profound, transparent and infinite. As long as you are attracted or repelled by anything the basic Love-Light eludes you. Hold all darkness and conflict inside the circle of this one all-pervading Light.

BE LIGHT

Visualize and feel a Crown of Light emanating from your head. Crown of Light says, "Be Light. Change dullness and darkness to light. Feel the radiance of your creative power."

Affirmation:
My aura is clear and shining with divine Light.

125 Aurora

With the aurora you can announce the hidden harmony of the rising Love-Light. The aurora is the dawn of compassion and the Light that transforms all suffering. You can now let go of both positive and negative, and gaze at everything with pure awareness. Your own cellular memories of conflict and suffering can be cleansed by meditating on this card and feeling the dawn of Love-Light within you. The rising sun of loving consciousness dispels all illusions, lies and confusions. You cannot grasp this Love-Light, but you can receive it as the dawn and give annunciation of its purity. Have the courage to announce this Love-Light through your own awareness of its infinite healing splendor.

ANNOUNCE THE COMING OF COMPASSION

Feel Aurora as a rosy dawn in your heart of hearts. Aurora says, "Awaken to the elixir of love within you and feel the ecstasy of loving whether you are loved or not. Realize that the dawn comes out of the darkness and is faint and fragile at first. Be gentle with yourself."

Affirmation:
I am coming into a wholly caring and compassionate life.

5 *Source*

The source is the cosmic Love-Light ocean from which everything originates and to which it all returns. This inexhaustible reservoir is here in a series of vortices which move through your chakras. The source within you is white Light containing specific vibrations of waves—from gravity and earth waves through heat and the visible rainbow to high frequency X-rays, cosmic, and gamma rays. Feel this source within you and become aware that every thought form rises from and returns to this Love-Light ocean like waves in the sea. Whatever trouble you may feel can be returned to the source by meditating on this card and experiencing the vortices of your chakras as specific color flow patterns of white Light. Let all of your pain or discomfort be churned in these wheels and you will feel an effortless freedom.

ACCESS SOURCE AND FOUNT FORTH

Visualize and feel the Source within you as a simple, cosmic, revolving energy. Source says, "Germinate. Change any stagnation and rigidity
you may have into a potency of your being."

Affirmation:
I receive inexhaustible cosmic energy through my wondrous body.

124 Being

You can now cease struggle, trying, and doing by realizing that your very presence is one with the source and all that needs to be done will be so without self-conscious effort or drive. Let go of all goals or results for the moment and immerse yourself in the limitless divine presence. Getting things done is an illusory self-centered view of what the universe accomplishes through you effortlessly. Suffering will cease when you release the idea that there is any self who is doing anything. Meditate on the afterimage of this card until you feel your own being in a wide expanse of space. The arising and disappearance of grass, earth, moons, and stars is renewed each instant in a pure state of being. Forever new and fresh, all doing can thus be fulfilled through this inexhaustible, spacious presence.

JUST BE

Visualize and feel Being as a state of communion. Being says, "The presence of the cosmos shines through you. Heal all apparent separations and find eternity in each moment. Change drive and pressure to pure acceptance of the ground of being within you."

Affirmation:
My presence alone is fulfilling and complete.

6 Cosmic Egg

You now have great potential for rebirth, or an emergence that is truly divine. If you feel you are about to burst, just realize that you are "pregnant" with something new. Your deep self is a seed about to   implode within you as a shining revelation of love. Just remain inwardly silent and still—even amidst the busy movement of your daily life. Then the mystery of the Cosmic Egg will be born within you. Enjoy the truth of your silent witness within. Cease trying to make anything happen. The Love-Light that is one with all things will emerge within you in its own time, rhythm, and way. Just be present and aware of the potential within and all around you while life's changes take place.

CONTAIN AND IMPLODE

Visualize and feel the Cosmic Egg surrounding you as a membrane that at once protects and expresses your essential being. The Cosmic Egg says, "Change impotency and explosive tendencies to quiet, contained, implosion. Incubate a new way of life within your shell."

Affirmation:
I am incubating a great idea, feeling, or form and have faith in its emergence.

123 Oneness

You are now one with everyone and everything through the Love-Light. Be aware how every thought, word, and action are resonate. This is not an amorphous merging, but awareness of the One Love-Light in everyone you meet. This Oneness allows you to know all you need to know when you need to know it. Trust yourself in the improvisational nature of life. Surrender only to the One from whence all response issues. Then your responses to other's needs will be clear, loving, and effective. Let go of any struggle with the many projects, duties, or objects in your life. As you return your awareness to Oneness, the multifarious aspects of life will sort themselves out. You are fully in all relationships through Oneness.

KNOW OTHER AS SELF AND SELF AS OTHER

Visualize and feel Oneness as a spatial tension in your heart, connecting you to the vast array of the cosmic structure. Oneness says, "Simultaneous synchronicities appear linear to the obscured doors of perception. Change fragmented views to an awareness of the symphony of cosmic harmony."

Affirmation:
I feel and know the One in every being I meet.

7 Movement

You can now flow with the invisible movement of the universe as you play with children, write an article, weed the garden, or talk to a neighbor. Whatever you are engaged in you can relax into a natural infoldment or unfoldment. Like the inhale and exhale of the breath, all movements are twofold—systolic and diastolic, in and out, birthing and dying. As you move through life, cease identifying with one side or the other. This one-sided activity leads only to hurt, frustration, and anger. Yes, grow, expand, develop, but remember that sooner or later, there will be death, contraction, and release. Be aware of the stillness of the Love-Light behind all movements and enjoy the dance you are engaged in. Be aware of the One behind and within all duality.

CHANGE AND INTERACT

Visualize and feel Movement within your cells and all through your being. Feel waves of power within you. Movement says, "Change isolation to interaction. Take action on your vision of the new."

Affirmation:
I move with the natural waves of the universe according to my inner needs and outer responses.

122 Flexibility

You can change roles, viewpoints, or strategies without compromising yourself. Allow yourself to feel the wholeness that contains all relationships as you generate a project, transform an identity you once thought real, or let go of attachment to a friend or relative. You can trust the Love-Light as you undergo change from the inside out. Flexibility is a mark of confidence in the essential. This does not mean forsaking who you are or being wishy washy. It simply means you can embrace more ways of the universe, empathize with more people and creatures. As you reach into unfamiliar territory of speech, role, or deed, realize that you become more whole the more you are able to embrace others.

MOVE AT ONE WITH ALL THINGS

Visualize and feel Flexibility as a field of vibrations in a joyous dance of possibilities. Flexibility says, "Stay centered and still and anything is possible. Change static thought into the revelation of infinite flux.
Each moment is a spontaneous play of energy currents in continuously changing forms."

Affirmation:
I am so confident in my wholeness that I can change my roles or viewpoints.

8 Infinity

Everything you think, say, or do in some way comes back to you in figure eight curves. You are already in the flow of life. The feedback of pain or pleasure is one way you learn. Now you can be aware that encouraging or resentful thoughts of long ago return to you, although you have forgotten the source. Also, you are conditioned by pain and pleasure. This limits you, whereas understanding of reality opens you infinitely. Your connection to the great mystery of infinity can be trusted as a potential to go beyond pleasure and pain to a true state of acceptance of what is real. As you accept, hold the space and embrace what you actually witness in your life. Then you enter the Love-Light that is within and yet beyond all conditioning. The infinite tides of in and out will spend themselves as you continue to hold the space of infinity.

RELEASE AND RETURN

Visualize and feel Infinity within your own being. You are open, and at once with all things through infinity. Infinity says, "Change limitation to infinite returns. You are abundance. Feel the waves of power returning to you infinitely."

Affirmation:
I let go of rigidity and go forth with faith in the flow of life returning infinitely.

121 Reverberation

Now you know intuitively that what is coming to you is the result of previous effort or neglect. You don't need to know results ahead of time, but only pay attention to what is actually happening and cease trying to make anything happen. You will be truly free and in the flow of the great mystery when you no longer want anything to be any different than it is.

Your relationships give you feedback on the past, but now you can live in a reverberating, alive present by simple unconditional love and acceptance. Cease trying to change the 'other' as well as yourself. You cannot improve on anything by effort and struggle, but you can reveal what is vibrating inside. This compassionate witnessing purifies reactiveness and confusion. Your essence reverberates throughout space.

PARTICIPATE IN MYSTERY

Visualize and feel Reverberation as the comic vibratory feedback of all you have sent out. Reverberation says, "Every wave of breath, feeling, and thought is still and equipoised in space. Behold yourself in the cosmos and the cosmos within yourself. Change isolated memories into the living feedback of the universe within you."

Affirmation:
My thoughts and feelings are a field of cosmic reverberations giving me feedback.

9 Guidance

Trust yourself to be a dowsing rod that can guide you each moment of your life. Your inner witness knows what your destiny is and how you can change useless habits into pure capacity. Simply watch your dramas without identifying with them. Orient yourself to the Love-Light within you and reflect on what it is to be human. Feel the energy rise in you as you release conditioning, controlling relationships, and work that harms you. You have something to offer humanity, like a seed that will germinate into harmonious action, when you learn to follow your inner guidance continuously. Sometimes you need to make decisions that take you one way or another. Cease forcing anything. Allow the decision to arise naturally within you. Trust the truth, direction, and discernment of your inner guide.

DISCERN AND FIND DIRECTION

Visualize and feel Guidance within you as the awareness that acts through you behind all appearances. Guidance says, "Change reactive judgement and blame to discernment and the capacity to be open to deeper guidance."

Affirmation:
I am receiving guidance from my higher Self each instant.

120 Peace

You may now feel the spilling over of the cup of well-being. Peace is the stillness and equipoise beholding the harmonies of the world, when you live in the nondual Love-Light. The more you accept other sentient beings as yourself, the more peace you will have. Though the suffering of others is not easy to be in the presence of, your inner peace will bring forth the Love-Light within others. Peace is the solvent of all ills. There is no possible defense against or elimination of suffering except through the Love-Light that embraces everything. Peace is a blessed embrace as you feel greater compassion for all beings. With each breath, breathe in the Love-Light, hold it a moment, as you more and more deeply enter the deep peace. Then all that is superfluous will move out transformed. With a peaceful presence you can guide others.

BE EQUANIMOUS AND SEE THAT ALL IS WELL

Visualize and feel Peace as the flower in your heart you have earned by cultivating equanimity. Peace says, "See the whole of life in clarity and balance. Your relation with others is non-reactive and serene. Change turbulent reactions to acknowledgment and honest witnessing. Persist forever with the awareness that peace lies within you."

Affirmation:
I feel more and more peace the more I embrace polarities.

10 Courage

Let go of daring or show, for now you have the courage to act naturally from a relaxed state. If you charge ahead out of zeal or fear, you will be cast into a reaction of feeling that you are being attacked. True courage is a centered capacity to receive guidance and go forth with whatever needs to be done. There is no need for heroic drama. Personal drama often is a distraction to disguise insecurity. Now is a time to face any weakness or insecurity while blessing yourself in the Love-Light that permeates and surrounds you. It takes greater courage to face your weaknesses and illusions than to conquer armies or rally people to an ideal. Let concepts and ideals go as you have the courage to face what is actually happening.

BE TRUE AND GO FORTH

Visualize and feel Courage within you welling up in your heart. Courage says, "Be true and go forth. Change cowardice, non-commitment, and passivity to courage.
Act on what you know to be true."

Affirmation:
I have the courage to be honest with myself and take action on my inspiration.

119 Actualization

You can actualize who you are in essence the more you embody the Love-Light. In daily life just realize that each moment that you are aware of what is and let go of attachments, you actualize yourself. This is not only a personal self. Cease projecting any ideas of what you want to do. Listen to and look at both the joy and suffering in your life. The more you allow the Love-Light to embrace the actual in daily life, the more you are able to actualize. This means doing by being. It doesn't mean doing nothing, but doing from a place of acceptance and love. The energy of actualization is powerful medicine to heal any sense of impotence or incompetence. Embrace other's woundedness as well as your own.

EMBODY THE UNMANIFEST IN THE MANIFEST

Visualize and feel Actualization as the recreation of your life according to laws of harmony. Actualization says, "Work with fear, denial, and pain as fertilizer for the cultivation of your true self. Change escape and fragmentation to a wise embrace of yourself."

Affirmation:
I am actualizing who I am each moment.

11 Order

The order in your life is in a perpetual flow from a center. Find the equilibrium point of zero within you and feel the dynamics of change move within you. You are a reservoir of memories through the cells of your body. Allow the akashic bank to reveal itself and speak of the order that is arising anew each moment. What is essentially happening to you is an unveiling of the inner order of your spiritual destiny. Let the old layers fly from you. The Love-Light lives within you in whole hierarchies of orders. Ask your higher self what is of greatest importance. Order your life according to your highest value. This may be a time when you "remember" the synchronous "lives" that appear to be past. This is alright as long as you don't attach to either the apparent positive or negative aspects. Watch the order from zero point—the center of all order.

STAY CENTERED AND PRIORITIZE

Visualize and feel Order within your whole being and your environment. Order says, "Harmonize and preserve. Change discord and disorganization to a new orientation. See the order inherent in your own body."

Affirmation:
I am centered and am ordering my life according to my highest values.

118 *Harmony*

You can now harmonize many disparate things, views, and aspects. The more you praise the One Love-Light through a continuous awareness of what happens in your life, the more harmony you will find. Harmony reveals itself through overtones and undertones of feelings, observations, and thoughts. The patterns of your life are a medley of possibilities that can manifest through sheer awareness. Allow yourself to be in a state of total wonder of people and events in your life. This wonder deep within you is one with the deep harmony of the universe—that radiates the colors of the stars, the lattices of crystals, and the music of birds. In this harmony, you are not separate from the harmonies of creation. You can draw out this harmony when you feel you are in dissonant, conflicting situations. You can heal and be healed.

BEHOLD THE WONDER AND HARMONY OF PATTERNS

Visualize and feel Harmony as music within your body and the body of nature. Harmony says, "Attune to the akashic imprints of your ancient past and release it into the present. Attune to the root of your conflicts in your unconscious and weed out distorted patterns."

Affirmation:
I hear the "music" in all things and reveal the harmony inherent in each situation.

12 Perennial Culture

The perennial culture is a spiritual current of harmonic order. The truth lives forever—sometimes underground, in wells, or the mainstream. Vortices originate from the one apex of Love-Light and spiral down into varied streams of culture through spiritual councils. You can be present at these councils now and can access whatever insight you need for the present. Be aware of the transmission of this perennial wisdom and you will be able to share riches with others. Let go of thoughts, words, and actions that interfere with the Love-Light. Streams and vortices of great culture are always around you. You need only be aware of them now, and receive this gift. Whether in conversation, gardening or music—this sharing of spiritual transmission is culture-making.

TRANSMIT WISDOM

Visualize and feel Perennial Culture as the transmission of wisdom from your spiritual ancestors through you. Culture says, "Access and transmit perennial wisdom. Change transient, short term, selfish values to wholesome values that empower you to be a leader to future generations."

Affirmation:
I drink of the stream of perennial wisdom and transmit its nutrients to those I meet.

117 Trust

Now you need to trust the unknown, the invisible aspect of the universe. Notice how the universe 'works' quite well without your doing anything! People come and go, events happen, the grass continues to grow in summer and die back in winter. Trust comes from the heart knowing that all is well. The universe plays! Sometimes you may be in difficult circumstances, but when you trust the deepest core of your being, you move through without unnecessary suffering. Trust yourself to know what you need to know when you need to know it. There are countless levels and dimensions of reality that we don't need to know. Let go of any defensiveness that comes from feeling you need to know everything. This is self-defeating. You are one with the universe. Trust.

HAVE FAITH IN THE UNIVERSE

Visualize and feel Trust as an innate confidence and peace in your heart. Trust says, "Be aware that the unknown has far greater power than the known. Change doubt to the certainty that the unknown source has the capacity to regenerate all things. Know that all is well just as it is."

Affirmation:
I let go of controlling, and trust my inner being and the cosmic interactions.

13 Balance

It is of the utmost importance now to stay centered and keep all your projects and relationships within appropriate limits. Equanimity comes from deep self-acceptance. As you reconcile your subconscious and conscious selves, and accept yourself more deeply, you will be able to stay in balance no matter what disturbances are happening. Deep breathing assists this balance—especially when being tested. Be aware of both sides of your body. Is your left or right side overly dominant? It will help if you do yoga or exercises that use both sides of the body equally. Perhaps too your energy is overly yang (strong, fiery, expansive, light) or yin (weak, watery, contractive, dark)? If so, give yourself exercises to complement the dominance. As you come into balance—physically, emotionally, and mentally, you will be able to embrace more and more of life.

FIND LIMITS, GROUND AND CENTER

Visualize and feel Balance as your deep center amidst the ever changing dynamics of life. Balance says, "Ground and center. Feel the deep connection with the earth in your body. Attune inwardly so that all extremes are in balance."

Affirmation:
I am living in complete balance of my right and left, masculine and feminine sides.

116 Wisdom

Wisdom embraces all opposites. Cease being concerned about attaining anything. Realize that wisdom is within you. This awareness is clear when conflicting desires and fears are released. Wisdom is being revealed within you as the capacity to embody the presence of Love-Light. How? Through a non-judgemental discernment of those thoughts, words, and actions that reveal the Love-Light and those that are reactive, self-defensive, and egotistical. The more you express your feeling in a safe place, the more you can surrender to the wisdom within you. In the face of strife or conflict, disease or confrontation, continue to be aware of what it is, while more deeply surrendering to the Love-Light. Wisdom takes great patience, humility, and simplicity.

EMBRACE OPPOSITES AND BE IN BALANCE

Visualize and feel Wisdom as the discernment of appropriate sources and means for a given effect. Wisdom says, "From the intangible to the tangible, your purpose is effected, but from the tangible to the intangible your purpose is sourced. Change clinging to results into a wellspring that you can apply in innumerable ways."

Affirmation:
With patience and confidence I trust the innate wisdom within me.

14 Divine Plan

You can now see the design of your energy and actions more clearly. The ten directions return to the center through your life force every moment. Be aware of the subtle energy through your spine from your feet to crown as the absolute column of your being. The eight horizontal directions are the arena of action. Allow your dreams and deepest subconscious states, as well as consciousness, to reveal to you the design—the divine plan. You have a purpose in life and the vibrations of this card can reveal it more than you now know. Get in touch with the energies that flow inward and outward and you will experience both what you receive and can be grateful for, as well as what you have to offer—in the great scheme of things.

BEHOLD AND DESIGN

Visualize and feel the Divine Plan all around you as a sacred circle. Divine Plan says, "Behold and design. Change mundane distractions to an overview so that you can see yourself in a greater perspective."

Affirmation:
My intentions are in harmony with the Divine Plan.

115 *Reciprocity*

You now realize that there is a give and take to life that has its rightful measure. Cease being disturbed if you feel you are giving too much or too little in a given situation. Reciprocity works over vast periods of time and in ways that cannot be measured by ordinary reality. What comes back to you is not always the same as what you give. The more you give with wisdom, the more you realize you are blessed with Love-Light. Outer manifestation may be translated into inner riches or vice versa—depending on whether you need more or less density or realization while you are in incarnation. The whole universe can be embraced as Love-Light within you. Your life is a gift and as you give of yourself with a clear purpose, you receive more Reciprocity within your life.

EMBRACE THE UNIVERSE IN YOURSELF

Visualize and feel Reciprocity as the natural rhythmic interplay between the Creator and creation. Reciprocity says, "You have received the gift of life, nurturing, friends, opportunities, and challenges. What resources are within you that you can offer to others?"

Affirmation:
I give the best that I am and receive great blessings.

15 Quest

You can explore freely now—especially if you are drawn in a direction that brings more inspiration and clarity in your life. If your quest takes you in paths of confusion, stop and find a way to rest deeply. Meditate and allow yourself to *feel*. As you feel, be aware of both positive and negative tendencies, peace or frustration, and anger. Let them come and let them go. Gradually your quest will become more clear in its direction. You may go through many relationships, feelings, and events before you realize the simplicity at the heart of the complexity. This simplicity is real the more your quest intensifies in feeling. Seek not more complex feelings, but a full body awareness of energy all around and within you. Your quest is to the heart of your true being.

FIND VARIATIONS ON THE THEME OF THE ONE

Visualize and feel Quest as your motivation to know the truth.
What form does your Quest take? Where will it lead you?
Quest says, "Question how the many come from the one and
how the many return to the one. What is the theme of your life
and what are the variations on this theme?"

Affirmation:
All my longings converge toward understanding myself.

114 Acceptance

You might as well accept how things are, for only then can you begin to make changes. Let go of attachments or a fixed, rigid idea of how you want them to be. Accept each moment as it arises and behold the wonder of possibilities. Your quest can cease in a deep release of expectations. Then the Love-Light reveals itself in the most surprising situations. Realize that nothing can be lost or found. Let go of a sense of gain and improvement, and look into the heart of what is. Be grateful even for the difficulties in your life. These are opportunities for dissolving old habits and cellular memory that is no longer relevant. Accept life as it presents itself to you. The Love-Light shines the more you accept. This is not resignation, but recognition and affirmation.

REALIZE AND ACCEPT REALITY

Visualize and feel Acceptance as a realization that, no matter how difficult, all is perfect and well. Acceptance says, "What needs to change and die will change and die. What needs to be reborn and grow will be reborn and grow. Change doubt to an awareness that all forms change, and that wanting anything to be other than it is subdues you."

Affirmation:
I affirm reality in each changing moment.

16 Sacrifice

You now need to prioritize—know what is truly of value—and give up all habits, things, and relationships that hinder your highest value. To sacrifice is to make sacred. Find what is sacred and subordinate everything else to it. Organize the rhythms of your daily life around the most important aspects of your life. What are you grateful for? How can you express your gratitude? Release any tendencies to grasp or gain—for they limit your possibilities to the confines of those tendencies. If something stands in the way of the offering of who you are in your essence, just recognize it and let it go. To make sacrifice is a deep pruning, a cutting away—so that the sacred can reveal itself all the more.

ACKNOWLEDGE THE SACRED

Visualize and feel Sacrifice as what you receive from God and the cosmos, and what you give back to God and the cosmos. Sacrifice says, "See the sacred in the earth and daily life. Change greed to gratitude and isolation to connection. Learn to give what others need to receive as much as what you need to give."

Affirmation:
I gratefully let go of habits that obscure the sacred.

113 Offering

You *are* the offering when you contribute who you are to life. Only you are uniquely you and no one can take your place. Offer yourself with integrity wherever you can. There is no loss in making an offering. You are the gift and the giver. Find your creative gift and trust that it is as much in being as in doing—and then find the way to offer your being. Realize that you have received your life as a part of creation. What you make of it is your creativity. Only your creativity—your unique manifest being—can be offered. For all else is not yours to offer. Each moment your breathe in the Love-Light you will make it your own and breathe it out for others. The divine receives everything that is truly offered and gives more Love-Light as a blessing.

OFFER YOURSELF TO CREATION

Visualize and feel Offering as the gift of yourself gathered in integrity and offered to all you meet. Offering says, "You are now fully individuated and can give appropriately to every situation. Change reluctance and uncertainty to the joy of being completely present."

Affirmation:
I offer my abilities, gifts, and being to the whole of life.

17 Intention

Your true intention is simply to be who you are. How can you get in touch with your primordial, authentic being? Focus and embrace. Be centered while incorporating more and more reality. Let your circle be as large as possible. The larger it is, the more you need to simply be. What you are will unfold. Trust the greater process. Let go of distractions and hold to who you are in every situation. The more quiet and steady the better. Think of every intention as a helper in your greatest intention of being who you are. The focal point is being a spiritual human. The tension is interior, the pressure is exterior. Include as many types of people (races, cultures, status, etc.) as possible in your circle, while remaining true to yourself. This is not being rigid, just being—then you can be flexible with diverse experiences.

FIND SOUL PURPOSE

Visualize and feel Intention centered in your heart of hearts and at once surrounding you as a sphere. Intention says, "Be in and move out. Change all tension to clear intention. Be here, now, relaxed, and attentive to the purpose of your life. What comes to you now?"

Affirmation:
I place all my gifts and efforts toward my life vow.

112 Consummation

You are finally truly burning through your karma. Your deep-est longing—to be who you are—is being fulfilled. There may be pain in the process or a lightening, but this is temporary. Consum-mation is a revelation of Love-Light as you breathe in and out each moment. All that you are not is fugitive and being burned away by spiritual truth. All that you are remains as a silent, essential witness of your many varied experiences. Review your life as if standing before death. This is a time to release and realize that you are not the sum total of your experiences, nor your body, feelings or mind, but are the Love-Light that never dies. In daily life, pay attention to what you no longer need, and let it go. Cease all defensiveness and open yourself to the living Light.

BECOME THE LIVING LIGHT

Visualize and feel Consummation as a wholehearted fulfillment coming out of unpredictable events in your life. Consummation says, "In the ash you shall be reborn. Rise like a Phoenix by working with the subtle energies all around and within you. Change self preservation to self revelation. Cling to nothing and allow."

Affirmation:
I am burning through all tendencies that obscure the fulfillment of my soul purpose.

18 Inspiration

Trust your inspiration and have the courage to take action on it. You are in a transition that is truly of the spirit. Let the spirit in and flow with it. There may be obstacles in going with the inspiration that challenge your steadfastness and courage to act on truth. Cease all hesitation, ambivalence—ifs and buts. Just be true to the inspiration. The more you doubt your inspiration, the less you will have. Your relationships, projects and work—all receive inspiration. Are you open to it? To remain alive, flexible and spiritually energized is to receive inspiration and take action. The fountain of inspiration within you is infinite.

BRING SPIRIT IN

Visualize and feel Inspiration coming into the crown of your head and down your chest. Inspiration says, "Breathe out dullness and confusion and breathe in pure light and spirit. What practices inspire you?"

Affirmation:
I trust the right inspiration in every situation.

111 Sublimation

    This is a time to make sublime, refined, and exalted your feelings and thoughts. Sublimation is a co-joining of spirit with all the more temporary aspects of life. It is *lived* inspiration—letting the Love-Light direct and guide. Allow yourself to be ground down, polished—so that high energy will resurrect you. Adoration, creative power and the energy of the cosmos are yours when you allow this fiery melting and dissolving. Your senses, too, are becoming more refined. Your perception is heightening and your energy is intensifying. Express how you feel. Be aware of the transition within yourself and the Love-Light will burn through all obstructions to being who you are.

MAKE ENERGY SUBLIME

Visualize and feel Sublimation as an elevation of all aspects of yourself. Sublimation says, "Pulverize and refine your life until you feel the constancy of the immutable in the mutable. Go through all changes as a purification and separation of the gross and subtle."

Affirmation:
I go through everything necessary to raise my life to sublime states of being.

19 Intuition

Spirit is moving within you. Feel it, trust it and your intuition will reveal astonishing things that are more real than many ways you are accustomed to. Follow the energy of your intuitive mind. Like birds in migration, intuition can be trusted to guide you to truth. Let go of doubt or of trying to figure things out. Intuition is born of spiritual fire. Allow yourself to feel intensely while being aware of the most subtle insights. Bring to awareness what is happening in your consciousness beyond your ordinary habits. Once you have an intuition you can unravel it with a state of open-ness. Surprise is a delight that can open new doors for you, and intuition is surprise guided by the higher mind.

FEEL SPIRIT ALL THROUGH YOURSELF

Visualize and feel Intuition circulating throughout your entire being and flashing inside your head. Intuition says, "Feel spirit everywhere. Change insensitivity to intuitive insight. Feel subtle energy of the spirit circulate throughout your entire being. Trust your own intuition."

Affirmation:
I am open to intuition in every situation, even if it runs counter to expectations.

110 Practise

Now you can deliberately absorb the suffering of the world and transmute it into Love-Light. Meditation, yoga, and good eating habits are all ways of practise, but the simplest and more effective is awareness of your self, and letting the truth shine through you. Practise is going through all doubt, hesitation, and fear of the void. Practise is awareness of each moment as it is happening, and clinging to nothing. Practise is clearing the debris of past belief systems. It is in incandescing matter by the light of the consciousness, which spontaneously becomes the bliss of the spirit. Create rhythms for your day that support your awareness and the energy of your body. The spirit shines through body, soul, and mind when your awareness becomes constant. Karma is thereby transmuted.

BE CONSTANT IN AWARENESS

Visualize and feel Practise as your conscious attention to the fires burning through you. Practise says, "Continue making an effort without thought of reward. Remain vigilant in all circumstances and identify with nothing that changes."

Affirmation:
I practise honest awareness about myself through compassionate witnessing.

20 Vision

As obstructions to clarity dissolve, you can be in pure vision. This is not visualization, but may begin with breathing and visualization of pure white light on the crown of your head. Visualize a six-petalled lotus. A pin point of light may spread out into the six directions filling your head. When the light is strong and clear, allow an image to enter. Let it change and change until only a pristine light remains, filling your head. Let it sink into your throat, heart, solar plexus, and lower chakras. Feel vision throughout your whole subtle body. Vision is a hologram of your pure spirit. When you purify your chakras with light, you will behold whatever divine image you need as a direction of your destiny. Vision is the sign and signature of your spirit.

SEE THE TRUTH OF SPIRIT

Visualize and feel Vision emerging from inside of your head.
Vision says, "Behold clear visions. Clear your being of
confusion to receive a direct vision from supernal realms
of your high self."

Affirmation:
My most pure and wholesome visions will become manifest.

109 *Suffering*

As you realize you are inherently interconnected with every other sentient being, you will feel both suffering and compassion. You are not alone. The poignancy of being in a sentient body is suffering. This suffering is the beginning of transmutation and the opening of your heart to feeling with others. This does not mean you will suffer more, but that you will realize how much all beings suffer, which in itself, will transform suffering into pure presence. As you allow yourself to *feel* suffering, your self pity will vanish into empathy. You are embedded in every living being, and every living being is embedded in you. The Love-Light transmutes suffering when you allow yourself to feel with others through your own suffering. Let suffering be pure energy. Let go of trying to possess it.

FEEL THE POIGNANCY OF EXISTENCE

Visualize and feel Suffering as the last vestige of clinging, a poignant burning within your being. Suffering says, "Feel and blend with everything and transmute negativity. Change pain into compassion. Bear with what comes to you and cling to nothing. What is immutable?"

Affirmation:
When I feel pain, compassion wells up in me and transmutes suffering.

21 Love

Momentarily you are in a whole state of love—which is the true nature of your soul. Your conscious mind may forget this loving state, but your deep being can never forget. Remain consciously in love as long as possible. If you feel you do not love, be still and go deeply within.

Quietly enter the triple flame of Love-Light and attune to your peak experiences: the people you love, the beauty of the mountains, ocean, or valley. Open the heart awareness that love is in the center of everything. Your soul knows all beings it touches through love. Go forth with love pervading your entire being as you behold everyone you meet. Express this love in simple ways: pressing a hand, a look, a smile, or tears of gratitude.

LOVE UNCONDITIONALLY

Visualize and feel Love within you and surrounding you. Love says, "Merge with me in an unconditional open state of pure being. Change possessive and conditional love to pure love. *Be* love."

Affirmation:
I share a state of open heart and pure love with everyone.

108 Resurrection

Your soul is now returning to its original pure state of love. Living who you are brings you more and more into *being* love. The resurrection of your soul may take the form of simple peace after powerful "death" experiences. As you slough off identification with subconscious reactive states, the pain and suffering are released. Then you live in a flood of energy. This energy is, in essence, love. As you listen inwardly you realize that everything—people, rocks, plants, and stars—is love in essence. The resurrection of your soul is a flood of spirit that underlies all synchronicity and meaning. You transcend evolution through this resurrection. You are coming home to love. Continue to be in a state of oneness with the Love-Light and all your true experiences are resurrected.

RETURN YOUR SOUL TO LOVE

Visualize and feel Resurrection as the reemergence of the original love in your soul. Resurrection says, "Face the invisible, the darkness, the downtrodden, and let love guide your soul through the circumstances surrounding you. Love is not blind, but enables the blind to see."

Affirmation:
I have suffered the consequences of desire and now my soul resurrects to pure love.

22 Desire

What you desire is a reflection of what you feel is lacking in your soul. Rather than possessing the "object" (person, thing, event) look within to find the root of the desire. Is your desire a subconscious reaction? Do you have desires that are in conflict? Conflictive desires indicate a reaction and splitting of your energy. Your soul is unified in love, but divided in desire. Since desire is the soul's inherent and natural agent, dream, observe, and witness how you suffer through different desires you have. Go within and find the root desire—the deepest longing of your soul—and find the relationship of the many small desires to this one big desire. Your deep longing is your soul's destiny to live who you are.

FIND YOUR DEEPEST DESIRE

Visualize and feel Desire within you as a longing for aspirations, and for taking on the qualities of the person facing you. Desire says, "Find out what you really want. Take on the qualities that others have. Change fragmented desires into a single unified desire in order to fulfill who you are."

Affirmation:
My greatest desire is to live an authentic life.

107 Responsibility

You can now respond to the reality of each living moment. The deepest desire of your soul—to be who you are—is being fulfilled. Now you can feel your oneness with other beings, responding simply and directly. This ability to respond opens you to the fullness of life, and releases the limited vantage of grasping and desire—to the miracle of love returned. Surrender to the Love-Light as you meet other people and situations. Your response to life will reveal itself in the delight of finding your whole being energized when you awake in the morning. Allow yourself to be sensitive to every situation as it arises and respond with the wholeness of your soul. Then every moment will be energized.

RESPOND TO EACH MOMENT OF LIFE

Visualize and feel Responsibility as your capacity to respond to life's changing circumstances. Responsibility says, "No longer are you driven by desires into tunnel vision. The field of your consciousness resonates to the most subtle events. The more you respond, the more your vision expands. The more you see, the more responsive you can be."

Affirmation:
Letting go of attachments, I respond to life situations as they arise.

23 Projection

The more you feel you have to possess someone or something, the more illusions you are weaving in your soul. This process of projection is to teach you how you are identifying with the object of your desire, but cannot actually see who or what it is. Look into the depths of your soul and let the masculine and feminine within you meet one another in internal dialogue. What do your feminine and masculine really want? Let them speak. Can you see that you have been projecting part of this dialogue on someone you want to be close with? Take another look at who they are. Do they really meet and fulfill the demands of your soul? If not, this may be because you are projecting and demanding rather than seeing the beauty of who they are with eyes of love.

LONG AND PROJECT

Visualize and feel Projection within you as an idealization of some person. See them as you want to see them. Projection says, "Behold what you long for. See others from the vantage of your own desire and project on to them what you need. Now realize how you blame others for qualities you refuse to acknowledge in yourself, and change this blame to self-acceptance."

Affirmation:
I look honestly at and take back my projections on to others.

106 Forgiveness

Now is a time when you can forgive yourself for projecting and demanding from others what you desired. You may have been hurt, frustrated, angry, or even spiteful and bitter. Accept these experiences and forgive yourself for these sufferings of the soul. You likely did the best you could. Now ask forgiveness of anyone or any being you have consciously or unconsciously hurt. Realize that your soul simply longs to eternally live in the Love-Light. To forgive yourself and others is to let the soul return to Oneness. Now forgive anyone and everyone who has hurt you. Instead of reacting and either recoiling or wanting revenge, go deeper into your soul and truly forgive them. They could only do what they did then. Now is a new opportunity. Let go of old wounds and forgive everyone involved. Your soul will be absolved.

MELT CHAINS OF SEPARATION

Visualize and feel Forgiveness as the release of hurt, blame, anger, and bitterness. Forgiveness says, "Open your eyes. Love sees everything and releases you from helpless reactions. Be grateful and accept yourself as you are. Forgiving others is then easy."

Affirmation:
I forgive myself and everyone who has ever hurt me and I ask forgiveness.

24 Shadows

The uncertainties of your life cannot be cleared by denying what hurts you. Your fears may be known or unknown, conscious or unconscious. It is now time to be aware that they exist whenever, in the past, you could not face the sources of pain, frustration, or anger. Shadows are our repressed and suppressed emotions. Shadows can be detected as resentment, hatred, or violent reaction to someone, or some condition. They also live in apathy, sluggishness, and a tendency to gloss over pain— or deep feeling of any kind. It is time for you to get in touch with shadows, for by feeling more and witnessing them in the Love-Light of your true being, they will surface and then be dispelled.

HIDE AND CREATE

Visualize and feel Shadows within your soul and all around you. See the person in front of you as the epitome of what you fear may be in yourself. Shadows say, "Hide and conceal what you fear and it may go away. Keep painful realizations repressed and deny any responsibility for pain or confusion. Seeing how you create your own shadows by repression, now ask to see your own blind spots."

Affirmation:
I ask to see what I previously denied and eat with relish all shadows of my soul.

105 Acknowledgment

Even though you may feel great suffering, you are now in a state to acknowledge that, in fact, you are suffering. In the past you may have denied *feeling* by distraction, glossing over, or being unconscious. Such denial only maintains the suffering through suppression. Now, by acknowledging it, you can *feel* again, and by holding whatever you feel in the Love-Light, suffering can be changed into clarity and peace in the depths of your soul. Acknowledge the truth of whatever is happening—without judgement. Pleasant or unpleasant, good or bad—has no relevance. Your soul is being cleared of very deep unconscious memories. The more you are neutral in judgement, the more you will be cleared.

ACKNOWLEDGE TRUTH

Visualize and feel Acknowledgment as the weight of karma in your soul. Acknowledgment says, "Behold the shadows of your past. Watch them change. Energy from the repressed desires are available to you now. How do you feel when you accept what you previously denied?"

Affirmation:
I now acknowledge past mistakes, ignorance, and hidden desires.
I seek to dispel shadows and illusions.

25 Human Image

You are now realizing that being human is a unique opportunity to experience all the kingdoms of life, as well as the stars, within your own being. Get in touch with your deepest longing. Your longing is, in some sense, to be whole, as an embodied human being. Your nervous system, sensations, heart, blood, and the cells of all your organs resonate to elements which are also in the stars and other planets. The image of the human vehicle is a profound wholeness. Trust that, since you have the gift of a human incarnation, you have both lessons to learn and gifts to give. As you discover your own wholeness and integrity more you will be able to transform lessons into gifts. The primary gift to you is a human body. With this gift you can give more of yourself.

LONG FOR WHOLENESS

Visualize and feel the Human Image as a seed-plan of divinity within your brain, heart, and abdomen. Human Image says, "Be whole. Go through fragmentation, fear, desire, and all self-images, to the root of the wholeness that is a divine conception within you."

Affirmation:
I am grateful for being born in a human body and I use it well.

104 Cosmic Body

You can now feel empathy with every living thing. As you expand your feeling of Oneness with everything, you will be able to bring healing and inspiration to everyone and everything you meet. The Cosmic Body is the directional force of creativity of the whole of evolution. You may feel a great resurgence of creativity in the energy of your being. Allow feeling to become insight and insight to become inspiration—for the direction of your creativity as well as empathy. Everything in creation has resonance. The more you feel this resonance, the more your own sense of wholeness will expand. By feeling the Love-Light in your Cosmic Body, the original divine human image will be fulfilled through you.

FEEL, EMPATHIZE AND EXPAND

Visualize and feel Cosmic Body as your body of truth, uniting all opposites within the metabolic rhythms of your organic body. Cosmic Body says, "Be true to yourself and in balance each moment. Allow sensations to be pure, attaching to neither good nor bad, pleasure nor pain. Say to yourself, 'I am alive forever!'"

Affirmation:
As I feel the resonance of creation in my empathic cosmic body, my creativity expands.

26 Genetic Code

Acknowledge and realize that your ancestors have gifted you, genetically, with exactly the capacities you need for your life. Your bodily qualities are a signature of your soul. The uniqueness of your body, your fingerprint, and psyche is a gift for you to use, explore, and receive feedback on. You need to appreciate evolution and time as well as synchronicity and eternity. Now is a time to progress in a step by step fashion in your growth of body, soul, and mind. Gratitude to your ancestors and fulfillment of your sexual longing with another you love is part of this process. So too is the possibility of a cleansing of traumatic cellular memory in your DNA as well as a transmutation of your DNA.

DIVIDE, UNITE AND TRANSMIT

Visualize and feel the Genetic Code as helical strands of a vine which is an umbilical cord to your personal ancestors and the ancestors of humanity. Genetic Code says, "Divide, unite, and transmit. Feel both separateness and the oneness with the ancestors within your very cells. Change isolation to succession and be aware of future generations."

Affirmation:
*I am grateful for my ancestors and trust my genes to code
my body processes.*

103 Incorporation

You can now go beyond the genetic characteristics given you by your ancestors through your empathic oneness with others. Your genetic code may change to entrain your cosmic body of Light now. The more you include others in the feelings you have, the more the Love-Light will fill you. Be as conscious as you can of how your body resonates to the whole body of the universe, which is the Body of God-Goddess. Include intention in your feeling of incorporating all sentience in your own body. The more you breathe in Love-Light, the more your genetic code will resonate to the whole. Empathy is the key to feeling this Oneness, which enables you to be responsible to other's real needs.

INTUIT AND EMBODY

Visualize and feel Incorporation as a larger sense of your family. Incorporation says, "Include all opposites in your way of life. Change resistance to all-inclusiveness. Bring many types of people and races into your heart. Endure each moment of exclusive limitation, judgement, and blame as preparation for accepting yourself more deeply."

Affirmation:
I incorporate all peoples and sentient beings in my awareness and empathy.

27 Body Systems

It is time to pay attention to your body. Listen to its messages. Notice the quality of any pains or unusual sensations. Bring Love-Light into your body and "massage" any irritating sensations with gratitude. Thank your body for alerting you to danger or illness. Your body is a wonder of chemical, molecular, structural, and perceptual processes that serve you day and night. Give thanks to your body and give permission to all your cells to release any toxicity or noxious matter. Your consciousness affects your body for good or ill. Be aware of the integrity of your body with your feelings and thoughts. There also may be an imminent change in your body processes now. Slow down and attune to your body and listen to what it has to say.

PROCESS AND CIRCULATE

Visualize and feel Body Systems of nerves, blood, muscle, bone,
respiration, and assimilation as an interconnected process.
Body Systems say, "Circulate and coordinate. Feel the
sensations of all your organs in harmony with each other.
Change lack of coordination in any system
to right connection and healthy rhythm."

Affirmation:
*I am grateful for all my body systems and give my cells permission
to be healthy.*

102 Vastness

The human body is patterned waves of Love-Light condensed into organic reactions that weave the body's cells. Now is a time when the aura of your many bodies (physical, emotional, mental, spiritual) is expanding and brightening. Allow yourself to feel empathy with all of life and the Love-Light inherent in life. As you do so, your sensitivity will be enhanced and each instant may be more alive. You also may feel a sense of spaciousness, experiencing the space between the atoms of your body. This is a time when you can realize that your physical body is inter-penetrated by more subtle bodies which have a more refined sense of reality than your identification with your physical body alone. As you come to be in contact with and trust these more subtle bodies, you will find that your identification expands to include all of sentient life.

EXPAND AND AMPLIFY LIFE

Visualize and feel Vastness as the limitlessness of your imaginal body. Vastness says, "Weave your way through the labyrinth of the world by compassionate empathy with all whom you meet. Change confinement and prejudice to openess and new vantages. Expand your point of view."

Affirmation:
I affirm the vastness of the universe and the multitudes of interconnections I feel.

28 Intensity

You may feel very intensely at this time. Go ahead and feel whatever it is, but release identification with any object of desire or even the intensity of feeling itself. Desire will amplify the intensity, whereas release will defuse it, and allow you to have more perspective while still feeling. Intensity is the power to perceive any illusion while being in it. Desiring any object is, in a true sense, an illusion, yet such illusions are an inherent part of learning. You can now learn what you feel most intensely about and the effect it has on your body. Be aware of whether the intensity is driving you or whether it is a feeling that energizes your life force to respond to life. Intensity can make you narrowly self-centered if you cease listening to life.

VIVIFY AND FEEL

Visualize and feel Intensity as the life-force throughout your body from head to toe. Intensity says, "Vivify and extend. Give attention to the sensations all through your body. Change isolated pain to an acceptance of intensity as pure sensation and energy. Extend this energy to all parts of your body."

Affirmation:
I feel the intensity of life while realizing identification changes.

101 Wholehearted

Now you are clearly open to life as it is and can be whole-heartedly one with your work, friends, projects, or whatever interests you. You can also be wholeheartedly receptive and then fulfill what you receive with a wholeness of directed energy. Open your heart and trust the unity of your being with the Love-Light. Wholeheartedness means being filled with bio-energy, life-force, prana, and following your heart-mind. If you are loving your work, loving your friends, loving life, you are wholehearted. Notice in what areas in your life, if any, you feel ambivalence or attachment. Release anything that is not in accordance with your true self and you will move into greater wholeheartedness.

BE TOTALLY PRESENT

Visualize and feel Wholeheartedness as a complete courageous fervor of your life committment. Wholeheartedness says, "Be still, center, and go forth without reservation. Cease holding back. Birth dedication out of doubt. Work for what you truly value."

Affirmation:
I am completely, wholeheartedly one with my life and all its projects in alignment with the whole of the universe!

29 Imagination

Use your imagination to reflect your true spirit. Visualize how you want your life to be. Now behold clearly, the Love-Light shining through your mind. Look to the imaginal plane where pure vision can reveal to you who you are and what you are capable of. Let the Love-Light pour through the crown of your head into the mirror of your soul so that projects you have and work you do are in complete accordance with the Love-Light. Let what you see become a visionary force guiding your soul and body, your aspirations and activities. If how you want your life to be does not conform to the Love-Light vision, ask again and again for guidance on how to transform your life.

BEHOLD REFLECTED IMAGES

Visualize and feel Imagination through your capacity to create images in your mind. Imagination says, "Reflect upon possible scenarios in your mind. Change literal, visual perception into imagined visions. How can you distinguish imagination from illusion?"

Affirmation:
I use my imagination to visualize the most wholesome life possible for me.

100 Receptivity

Now you can open yourself completely to the Love-Light. Release limited identity and any sense of control. Being receptive is the feminine power of the heart-mind in attention without focus. Be aware with a peaceful ease and trust in the all-embracing Love-Light of God-Goddess. In this state you become a pure vessel that is at total oneness with the elixir of the Love-Light. This receptivity is a communion with the divine through the synchronization of your heart and mind. This also means being receptive to others—how they are, more than what they say or do. Can you receive them as they are without judgement? Hold any unwanted patterns in the Love-Light and let them go. Now you can deeply receive and accept yourself.

ATTEND OPENLY

Visualize and feel Receptivity as the great openess of your heart-mind to the changes of life. Receptivity says, "Your own blood is illumined with the influx of divine Light as you purify your mind. Let fantasies and delusions go. Give thanks for the fullness in your heart."

Affirmation:
With unified heart, mind, and feelings, I am open and receptive to divine guidance.

30 Reason

There are times when you need to use reason and logic. In the world of time and space, reason mediates the preservation of life through the practical mind. Reason may also become very abstract. Reason is useful but it is well to realize its limits. When you reason, you are trying to understand life in terms of cause and effect, and linear sequence. If you have a project that needs careful management, use reason in a step by step progression to attain an aim. Alternately you may want to know the cause of something that has already happened. Examine the chain of events backward until you find the cause. Reason is beneficial for control, but not for releasing control and opening to the Love-Light.

PUT IN AND FIGURE OUT

Visualize and feel Reason through your rational and logical mind. Reason says, "Change rationalization to sequential thinking. Think in a step by step, logical manner in relation to events of the world."

Affirmation:
I can use reason when I need to perform practical and logical actions.

99 Brilliance

Now you can receive truth through the Love-Light in a flash of the higher mind. You can trust your direct perception of self and others and shine the Love-Light through your heart-mind. Have the courage to live what you see, how you see a new paradigm. Your brilliance will increase the more your release mind games, such as disguise, distortion or camougflage. Brilliance is a flash of awareness that goes beyond reason to paradox: the oneness of two opposing ideas. You can now live in contradiction, for there is no contradiction when the brilliance of your mind embraces opposites. Seek not to figure anything out, but be a loving witness to polarities and your brilliance will shine.

SEE AND SPEAK CLEARLY AND DIRECTLY

Visualize and feel Brilliance as the natural light of your heart-mind. Brilliance says, "Find the infinite in the finite and allow yourself to be a beacon in the fog and darkness of the world. Let wandering thoughts go and behold the light in the forms of all things."

Affirmation:
Brilliance shines through my heart-mind when I embrace opposites.

31 Memory

The imprints in your mind and DNA from cellular experience are often very deep. Now is a time to go into any repetitive patterns that you no longer need, patterns that may have been a defense around some part of you that was wounded. Hold a space of loving witnessing while you *feel* these defensive patterns. Just watch and let the memory go. It will eventually change into a clear space in your mind. Your memory is useful in areas of practicality—to know where you put things, to remember a verse, or an incident. But let go of any judgement around these memories. The less judgement—even around very intense negative memories—the more you will actually be able to remember. The human mind has a whole racial memory buried within it.

RECORD AND PLAY

Visualize and feel Memory through a recollection of past experiences. Memory says, "Change distorted or blocked memory to vivid recall. Remember what you previously denied and didn't want to be true. Remember when you hid, lied, or masked reality. Remember the beauty of reality."

Affirmation:
I can remember anything that is relevant to my wholeness and can release the roots of traumatic memories.

98 Poetry

Now you are clearing your mind of judgement around memories to a degree that you see greater meaning in your life. Making meaning of memory is poetry. Your life will become poetry the more you open yourself honestly and humbly to the meaning of events in your life. You may ask: "Why did that happen?" If you honestly reflect on the aspirations and fears you had that led to a certain event, you will glean greater meaning. The heart or core of any matter is meaning that, when seen in the Love-Light, becomes poetry. Are you open to digging to the roots of your memory—events you've forgotten perhaps from pain? Let your mind become a repository of the meaning of your experiences. Fuse heart and mind through self-acceptance.

DISCOVER HIGH MEANING

Visualize and feel Poetry as the deep flowing utterance of your heart of hearts. Poetry says, "Speak the mystery you have heard only in your heart. Reveal the river flowing through your own life. Speak your mind."

Affirmation:
I transform my memories into meaning and find the poetic essence of all I have lived.

32 Thought

Being true to who you are, allow your thoughts to be an easy, relaxed process of reflection. Cease trying to analyze anything you are anxious about. Give up results for now and focus on the present thought-moment. Reflect on what is actually happening to you and what is unfolding from within your mind. Concentration is good, but so is open awareness without any fixed focus. Let your mind go through the process of beholding thoughts and letting go of all ideas that are not resonant with your purpose. If you feel you have no purpose, just watch your thoughts without attachment and see how thoughts fulfill themselves and then dissolve. Your purpose will be revealed without your trying.

CREATE A MENTAL WORLD

Visualize and feel Thought as the creation of an idea. Thought says, "Reflect deeply on a problem. What do you want to know? How can you go about finding out? Generate questions and ideas on solutions."

Affirmation:
Holding my intention, I allow my thoughts to emerge and let go of thoughts interfering with my soul purpose.

97 Insight

Now you are becoming so practical in detached thinking that it is no longer thought, but insight. Right and left hemispheres function as one for you now. Sudden insight is a direct perception of Reality. This is only possible now that your mind has been entrained by your heart. Let heart and mind be one. Your understanding can now go beyond ordinary thinking. Insight emerges when the Love-Light flashes through your heart-mind. It may be sudden or continuous, depending on your ability to sustain the creative synthesis of all opposites. Then your heart-mind is still, clear, open, and able to reflect the highest divine Ideas through the Love-Light. Behold your true being in the divine thought of Love-Light and you will have all the insights you need.

SEE HEAVEN IN A SEED

Visualize and feel Insight like eyes opening within every cell of your body. Insight says, "Be the eye, the light, and the object seen. Change the duality of subject and object into an 'ah ha!'"

Affirmation:
Insight comes to me when my whole being seeks understanding.

33 Vortex

You are coming into a new swirl of possibilities. Be still and centered, for otherwise you might be whirled into anxiety, uncertainty, or attachment. The vortex is the spiritual center of nature within you. It is being in touch with the force that energizes the whole cosmos. The vortex is in the center of every star and planet, as well as within your own cells. It has a positive and negative polarity that makes the vortex rotate or vibrate. If you can hold the positive and negative together in one spiritual energy—a space of neutral awareness—then you will find the center of the vortex. Being aware of the inhale and exhale of breath can assist this, for they follow naturally upon one another, and your awareness need neither judge nor be attached to one side or the other.

BE CALM AND DETACHED

Visualize and feel Vortex as a great spiral in the turning of the sky around the pole star and the turning of the earth on its axis. Vortex says, "Spiral in and out. Change transcendent states to dynamic involvement and participation in life. Pivot and dance in centered cycles."

Affirmation:
I can hold the centerpoint of awareness amidst changing energies.

96 Sound Current

The Music of the Spheres is within you when you listen to the quality of each tone you hear. Listen to another's voice or your own. You will notice when there is a dissonant quality. Then you can receive it with your consciousness and gradually entrain the dissonance to resonate in harmony. Sometimes there may be a gap or breaking of the voice. This may indicate correspondence with a chakra that needs opening or clearing. Invoke the Love-Light and allow sounds to come from your voice. Emotional charge of painful past experience can be cleared from your cells through toning. Try all the different vowels in a series of tones. Notice which vowels or tones you feel harmony with. As the sound current enters into your voice, disturbances will be cleared.

RECEIVE UNIVERSAL HARMONIES

Feel and hear Sound Current as the primal sound coursing
through your life in streams of vibrations. Sound Current says,
"In the silence, receive the one flowing surge of sound that
transcends time. Listen to the vibrations
of all things within yourself."

Affirmation:

*By sounding Om or HU in sustained tones I can harmonize my energy
with the cosmic sound current.*

34 Resonance

You can now be attuned to the natural rhythms of your life. Whether or not you feel resonant with your partner, friends, work, or home, this is a good time to be more sensitive to how you really feel. Be honest with yourself. To acknowledge your feelings is the first step. Find the source of any discomfort or pain in yourself and hold it in your body. Now feel how it is to be with your partner, work or whatever the issue may be. Do they resonate with your pain? Do they resonate with the peace you have when you feel happy? You may need to release attachment to habits that keep you whirling in a vicious circle before you can do this. Allow yourself to resonate to everyone you meet—for this is how you attune to your true presence.

VIBRATE AND HARMONIZE

Visualize, feel and hear Resonance as the harmony of vibration in all things. Resonance says, "Be one with everyone and each thing you meet. Change disengagement to connection. Change dissonance to resonance."

Affirmation:
Through resonance I can discern what is for my highest good and what is not.

95 Listening

Listening to your heart is a way to hear the Music of the Spheres. It is a good time to listen to others also. What do people really mean in their hearts? Often people's words are not what they mean. Can you hear behind the words? Listen to the tones within them and discern what they mean in their essence. As you listen more you can clear yourself of chatter, needing to know, and anxiety. Listen to your deep heart. Listen, listen, listen until you *feel* who you are. Then you can really say or sing what you mean. And others will more easily understand you and be able to match heart and word, mind and voice. The Music of the Spheres comes through all things: stones, plants, people, and planets, when you truly listen.

LISTEN AND CLEAR

Feel and hear Listening through your ears as an open receptive state in your mind. Listening says, "Clear interference and static. Change insensitivity and noise to sensitive, open receptivity. Can you hear the meaning of things?"

Affirmation:
I am listening in order to hear the essence of things.

35 Time

The more you realize time is a rhythmic cycle the more you will free yourself of being driven by it. Time is a process for you to have many experiences so that you can understand yourself more deeply. Time also helps to regulate your life in harmony with natural rhythms. Time can be an easy flow, organically unfolding daily processes of sleep, meditation, exercise, eating, work, play, and love-making. The more fully you accept life's daily rhythms, the less aware of time you are. If you feel pressured by time, slow down, stop and look within. There may be an old wound, emotional pain, or trauma that is driving you. The race against time is the fight and flight response to danger and hurt. Feel it and let it go and you will realize the timeless quality amidst the rhythms of daily life.

REGULATE AND MAKE RHYTHMIC

Visualize and feel Time as a pathway running only in one direction, carrying you from conception to birth, youth, adulthood, old age, and beyond. Now feel Time as a cycle in which you reincarnate through many lifetimes. Time says, "Pass through and pass beyond. Regulate and make rhythmic. Change the immutable to a state of transformation. Enjoy the changing phases of your life."

Affirmation:
I feel timeless when I enjoy the rhythmic unfoldment
of each moment in daily life.

94 Constancy

Are you reliable to yourself? Constancy is the capacity to know your unconscious mind and emotional nature enough to be aware of your ability to fulfill your commitments or devotions. There is no point in having high ideals if you can't practice them. Now is a time when you can take a small step each day in setting your sights on a place you can reach. It is important to put to daily practise what you believe in, value, and speak for. Your constancy then is firm in your relationships as well. Let the Love-Light be nourishment each moment as you consistently take daily action on a direction you have chosen. Use time wisely by allowing enough time for everything you seek to fulfill. Inner constancy comes through a kind of music that inspires you each moment, in each step of the way, until you become part of the universal flow.

INVOKE CONSTANT PRESENCE

Visualize and feel Constancy in your heart as the power to fulfill what you say. Constancy says, "Invoke presence continuously. Find the rhythms of the universal order. Change erratic and inconsistent tendencies to reliable ways to go forth."

Affirmation:
I follow through on commitments I make to myself and others.

36 Star

Divine Love and Light is everywhere shining through stars. You also have a star quality through the radiance of your aura. Realize that the Love-Light of God is central in your heart, which is also one with the central intelligence and love of the stars. The more you live and embody truth and love, the more clearly your aura shines. As you feel and face your fears and hold them in the Love-Light, they will be dispelled and thereby the obstructions to your star presence will be melted away. Your star presence is a vibratory link with the stars which your own aura resonates to. The more intensely you feel, the more energy you will access to dispel any confusion, repression, or block to the pure radiance of the Love-Light through your being.

RADIATE

Visualize and feel Star as the radiance of your own being while you burn through the potential of your life destiny. Star says, "Radiate and shine. Change your innocent, formless being into a centered energy that longs to return to its source through light."

Affirmation:
I feel love for all beings and radiate to others my inner light.

93 Concentration

Now is a time to focus—to bring to a united center any disparate issues or energies. Cease dissipating your attention and energy with distraction and running after things. Concentrate on the Love-Light within your being, allow whatever arises as thought or feeling, then be released. The more clear you become, the more your concentration will be strong and yet peacefully balanced. Your deep monadic presence is one with the galactic center which contains the hologram of the whole galaxy. By concentrating on the Love-Light within, your vibrational connection to the galactic center is opened and you can "tune in" to whatever you need to know. To concentrate to this degree sometimes bring pain from old wounds that are ready to heal. Realize how healing crises come from a concentration of energies.

FOCUS INNER ENERGY

Visualize and feel Concentration as the power to focus your whole mind. Concentration says, "Be still, centered, and at one with things. Change distraction and confusion to a single point of attention. See the One in each and every thing."

Affirmation:
I concentrate my energy in different centers for attunement and healing.

37 Sphere

  This card reveals to you that you are entering into the sphere of the imaginal realm. This may take the form of significant dreams, visions, or synchronous events. You may suddenly realize what certain symbols mean or be able to read events—like the flying of birds, the arrival of certain letters at the same time, synchronous phone calls, or the falling of a tree. The Sphere is like a seed. It has potential through the patterns of meaning, but it is not fully manifest. It may come to you as an idea or awareness that you felt dimly before, but now see clearly as a source to act on. It is well to allow yourself incubation time now, and let the imaginal space to unfold within you. Contain the images and ideas you have and refrain from getting distracted. Trust your own deep processes.

INCUBATE SEED-IDEAS

Visualize and feel Sphere surrounding you, bringing a sense of peace and potency. Sphere says, "Incubate seed-ideas and allow your imaginal body to surface in a waking dream. Transform the void of emptiness into imaginal possibilities.
What do you see?"

Affirmation:
I remain a silent witness to inner processes and images
until they are ready to be born.

92 *Awakening*

You can more fully awaken now from the unconscious and subconscious dreams you have had. The Love-Light within you knows you. Now it is time for you to know the Love-Light as a kundalini energy rising from the base of your spine, up through your chakras, and out of your brow and crown. This is also an awakening to creativity. It is a wake up call to live who you really are. You can see the many ways you have been asleep and functioning only partially. This "sleep" is shattered now, and it may be disturbing to you. Open yourself to this greater Reality even if it is shocking to you. It is time to realize that life is more multidimensional and alive than you've ever imagined. Awaken to as much as you can—for you contain the whole body of nature in your own body. Energize with the dawn and be empowered.

AWAKEN TO REALITY

Visualize and feel Awakening as a lightning bolt of divinity in a storm of confusion. Awakening says, "Awaken from dreaming and come into lucid awareness. Change unconsciousness to complete consciousness of all aspects of your being."

Affirmation:
I am awakening to hidden images and energies and am open to letting them burst through any narrow world views I have.

38 Dimension

Now you can access dimensions beyond the perceptual three dimensions of space. Dimensions divide the unity of the Love-Light into multiple realities. But to find a medicine, a pattern, or sacred art for a particular person in a particular situation, you need to be able to be specific about the dimensions needed. Dimensions are the means by which seed-ideas are projected into potential manifestation. You may have an image or idea that you need to manifest. Be aware of whether it is a material, psychic, or spiritual dimension that is appropriate for its formation in space. Sometimes a more subtle dimension will have a greater impact and sometimes it takes a physical spatial dimension to reveal what is needed.

UNFOLD DIMENSIONS

Visualize and feel Dimension above, below, to the right, to the left, in front and behind you. Imagine multiple dimensions folded inside of you. Dimension says, "Unfold dimensions from your center outward so that the possible can change into form. Change randomness and confusion to awareness of new dimensions."

Affirmation:
I can discern what dimension is relevant for a given problem or issue.

91 Surrendering

You may be experiencing some difficulty—sleeplessness, obstacles to your intent—trials of any kind which are peripheral to the real issue. Surrender to the divine Love-Light and all else will take care of itself. Surrender to the One only. Perhaps you feel subtle energy rising up your spine. Allow this flow and purification of your being. Release all relative efforts to control—either yourself or others. Control is not power. Trust the inherent stream of divine Love-Light. Let go of control and manipulation. Cease running after anything and enjoy the presence of other beings around you: birds, flowers, people, animals. You are awakening more every day the more you surrender to the divine One. At this time, every effort to do anything is likely a distraction. Let it all go and see what emerges. Kundalini energy is flowing through you.

SURRENDER RESISTANCE TO AWAKENING

Visualize and feel Surrendering as the yielding of resistance to the surge of energy streams. Surrendering says "Ground in truth and trust. Release the useless waste in your life. Change stubborn willfulness to responsiveness. Be poignantly present while yielding to the impulse towards oneness."

Affirmation:
I am surrendering my attempt to control—myself, others, or situations—and am consequently being empowered.

39 Space

You need an arena for the sacred in your life. Find or create a space for communing with divinity. This may be physical space or psycho-spiritual space. There is no hierarchy in this space, but there is a quality of intimacy, deep quiet, and balance. Let the eternal live in you through this space. Allow images to appear in this space if they want. Notice which images or feelings draw you toward the eternal. If you are seeking to heal a relationship or find a form for a particular project, put your intention into this space and let the solution emerge. Don't try to make anything happen, but allow the solution to appear in the sacred space. It may also be that you need more space to find your way. Go to the country and take a long walk, or change your working or living space. Create the right spatial conditions for the Love-Light to manifest in you.

EXPAND AND FEEL SPACIOUS

Visualize and feel Space within you and all around you. You are as permeable as space is. Close your eyes and ears to the outer world. Space says, "Become spacious and invisible. Change contraction and limitation to expansiveness. Feel space opening within you as vast possibilities.
Be aware of an imaginal space opening before you."

Affirmation:
I am creating an inner and outer space in accordance with my needs.

90 Flowing

Now you can really flow. The Love-Light is becoming a creative energy for you—for it is stimulating and awakening the unconscious in you. The whole stream of evolution is in your energy body, and if you feel pain anywhere, it is an area to embrace with your consciousness. Ancient memories of suffering can now be released. Remember, the Love-Light can heal all, and its pervasive presence through your being can liberate you. You need to flow on all levels now, for hanging on to anything fixed will only bring more pain. Allow yourself to feel and flex. The kundalini in you is rising. Feel it as a release of any rigid idea of who you are. A natural flow of evolutionary energies will rise in your being and bring you to a new creative level of being.

FEEL COSMICALLY CREATIVE

Visualize and feel Flowing as the rising sensations of ancient memory and primal energy. Flowing says, "Feel surging evolution rise within you. Change rigid habits to a momentum of creative consciousness and power."

Affirmation:
I am receptive to cosmic energies and creatively flow with them for my highest good.

40 Form

Now you can bring forth or recognize a form from the dreams you have been incubating for years. Trust the form you see in your dreams or imaginal space. You can bring forth the sacred in a form that is transferable to others. Go into the depths of your being and behold the form that will fulfill your dreams. This is sacred art. Don't hesitate to explore forms of art, gardening, music, or dance that you have never exercised before. You can manifest the new forms you see by gathering materials that can be used to reflect the form: beads, seeds, color, a flute, or wood. What we think of as substantial matter is not the form, but can manifest in form. Be as true to the inward form you see as possible.

PERCEIVE THE OUTER THROUGH THE INNER

Visualize and feel Form as the finite answer to your imaginal need. Form says, "Behold the form of what you imagined possible. Change formlessness and chaos into a specific form. Bring forth sacred art from your own experience."

Affirmation:
I am finding a form and body for my vision and love.

89 Transformation

You are in the beginning of a major change of energy levels. For this transformation to occur, you need to allow the depths of your feelings to emerge. This is an opportunity for a great healing. You can now heal through dreams and visions that reach down into cosmic depths. This plunging into the unconscious deeps is not necessarily easy. Your psyche has layers of experience, some of which may still be in unresolved pain. Let the Love-Light flow through and transform you. This implies letting go of outworn forms and habits and trusting that the divine source will support you in this next phase of your life. You need to live the Love-Light, that is, fully embody it, for this to happen. Just be aware and allow.

REACH DEEP AND ALLOW TRANSFORMATION

Visualize and feel Transformation as the power to change your energy, thoughts, and actions. Transformation says, "Reach down deep and allow yourself to feel the energy in your body. Penetrate and unveil. Change static form into a streaming current."

Affirmation:
I am going through and embodying many energy changes with confidence in the source.

41 Energy

You may be feeling the energy in your body now as a source of exuberance. This energy is a treasure from the cosmos for you to use wisely before you die. Yet death is part of the process of life wherein energy distributes itself differently. In death, atoms and molecules are simply a dance, whereas in life, they weave cells and tissues. Be aware of the great value of energy in your body. As your gratitude increases so will your energy. Energy is the source of change and transformation, and is the universal exchange system. If you are feeling a lack of energy, be still and just feel the sensations in your body. Bring full awareness to these sensations—whether painful or pleasurable—and let them be pure sensation without judgement. Now focus your attention and breathe from your abdomen in the space behind your navel for at least ten minutes. As your awareness intensifies, so will your energy.

ENERGIZE AND ENLIVEN

Visualize and feel Energy flowing through your entire body. Energy says, "Energize and enliven. Feel waves and pulses of energy all around you. Dissolve the outworn in your life and release old self-images. Dance yourself awake!"

Affirmation:

I am grateful for the energy I feel and enhance it through conscious breathing.

88 Essence

Your essence is the unification of energy and matter through consciousness. Your cells want to be felt, acknowledged, and allowed to heighten their vibration until the essence of your true being shines. Essence is the spiritual quintessence of matter through your Light-Body. As you receive the Love-Light more and more, it transforms energy into essence through a cooperation of your deep intention and your DNA. Cease doubting that mind has an influence on matter. You can trust your experience of heightening vibrations in your cells. You can trust the influx of Love-Light in your being initiating radical changes you may be feeling now. No one said enlightenment was easy or painless! Realize that if energy is being withdrawn, it is to refine your awareness of the most minute changes in your cells. They are opening to the Love-Light in stillness. Essencifying is an interior activity, not an outer expression.

DISTILL AND REFINE

Visualize and feel Essence as the butterfly flight of your light body. Essence says, "Transmute and refine. Emerge and fly. Change all raw energy into the pure essence of your being. Your essence is a light-body."

Affirmation:
I trust the refining energy I feel and receive more Love-Light in my cells every day.

42 Mass

You may feel heavy and dense now because you have identified with the physical world. Don't forget that even matter is made up of a spacious dance of atoms and molecules. This is actually a good time to embody or manifest something you have been imagining. It is also likely that you can manifest money or other material things of value. Then give what you love a body. If you get too attached to matter—whether as money, objects, or your body—you will likely limit your capacity to energize, find directions and clarity. However, you can now create a grounded foundation for a project, or find a way to manifest a very practical situation. Realize that all of matter is one vibrating mass.

ACCUMULATE AND STORE

Visualize and feel Mass within your bones and flesh. "Mass says, "Accumulate and store density. Contract and hold on. Change energy and dissolution into mass and embodiment. Feel the massiveness of your own body and the tangibility of objects. What can be more real than this mass?"

Affirmation:
I appreciate matter as spirit dancing and I manifest out of love.

87 Gathering

You can now gather your deep essence together through a process of inner awakening and receiving more and more Love-Light. Gathering is a mutational power of nature and spiritual process of cellular lightening. This is not a time to be outwardly active but inwardly aware of your cells. Appreciate how they have worked and nourished you all of your life. Give them permission to release all toxins and outworn or reactive, negative thought-forms. Open them through your consciousness to drinking in the Love-Light. The more they receive this nourishment directly from the divine One, the less they need of food—except pure, organic fruits, grains and vegetables. Visualize the Love-Light coming in with each breath. You might also gather a few friends and pray and meditate, being conscious of breath together.

GO WITHIN AND GATHER ESSENCE

Visualize and feel Gathering as an embodiment of your true being, curled like a chrysalis. Gathering says, "Gather, spin, and weave your essence. Change confusion and density to a gathering of your light-body. Gather the disparate parts of yourself into an integrated whole."

Affirmation:
I am gathering friends and values that are in harmony with the Love-Light.

43 Inertia

You may resist change of direction now and be in a groove of some success, but it is well to remember that all things inert have no potential for growth or mutation. You may be in a status quo job or be following the norm in society to a degree that makes it hard for you to actualize your true being. Examine your societal and childhood conditioning and realize that you can choose to do something different. This may take courage as well as incessant practise. Changing habits is sometimes like training a wild animal. Be open to a radical change of direction. Let your past die. Your present is formed out of habits of the past, but presence is formed from an oblique change of habits toward the eternal present, living moment. On the other hand, you may be in a momentum along a path that will change of its own accord. Just watch, wait, and be.

HAVE MOMENTUM AND CHANGE DIRECTION

Visualize and feel Inertia within your blood. Inertia says, "Resist change and become heavy with gravity. Continue the momentum of your habits and you will resist change. Now transform change itself into resistance to change. The momentum of certainty changes death into rebirth."

Affirmation:
I allow momentum where my habits support my highest good and change my habits where they do not.

86 Fearlessness

The universe is in your cells. Call yourself forth fearlessly, in the face of convention. The universe is tending towards a spiritualization and lightening, and your fearlessness is needed to change the resistance of old, outworn habits. This could be a time of rest from outer work and responsibilities. For you need to go deep within and face all your fears—of the unknown, of being controlled, of being a victim, of madness, or death. You may have vigilant or conscious sleep at this time. The vibration of your cells are changing to be more open to the Love-Light. When fearlessness is mastered you have gone through your conditional fears and accept more fully the uncertainty and mystery of life. Free yourself of expectations and live from a place of unconditional love. Fearlessness nourishes your light-body.

PASS THROUGH FEAR

Visualize and feel Fearlessness as a whirling wheel that spins from your innermost being. Fearlessness says, "Witness the unconscious. Change doubt, denial, and fear into acceptance. Be vigilant and awake when you sleep. Face and move towards what you fear. How can you move through?"

Affirmation:
I acknowledge and face fears and by releasing fear of not being loved, I live in unconditional love.

44 Direction

It is imperative to find direction in the whirl of the world. You cannot find direction merely by taking what appears to be the best opportunity. The direction that emerges from the change of past outworn habits must be motivated from within yourself. Find what intrinsically gives you joy, or what you truly feel is right under the circumstances. The direction you take has everything to do with living who you are. You could lose yourself if you don't *embody* and live the direction in greatest harmony with your true self. This card also indicates that you have the material means to sustain the direction you choose. Resources are or will be coming. The most important thing is to be true to the direction that is unique to you. Follow it through. Make a dedication in the direction you choose and don't be deterred by other people's opinions.

LET INTRINSIC JOY GIVE DIRECTION

Visualize and feel Direction stirring within you for revitalization and renewal. Direction says, "Accept change and work with it to manifest what you need. Polarize and depolarize the multiple tendencies within yourself. Enter the center of who you are and manifest your reality."

Affirmation:
I choose to direct my life according to the most wholesome, unified values.

85 Remembering

You no longer need a map of where you are going, for you have a vibrational memory in your cells. Atoms remember their birth in the sun and subatomic "particles" remember their birth in the origin of the universe. You remember your vow, dedication, and purpose when you are wholehearted. Remembering the pure state of being within enables your energy, and even possibly your DNA, to change more in accordance with your true self. In so far as you have forgotten what your deep being knows—of beauty, truth and love—it is more difficult for the Love-Light to nourish your cells. Remembering is bringing into oneness what the Love-Light eternally issues as the elixir of life. Relax and remember by trusting the Oneness. Your light-body is being reborn as you release obscurations to Love-Light.

REMEMBER WHO YOU ARE

Visualize and feel Remembering as the process of returning to the source and purpose of your being. Remembering says, "Allow and recall, release and remember. Change blocks and amnesia to clear, lucid awareness of who you are."

Affirmation:
I remember my essence and gifts, and am applying them to my soul purpose.

45 Planet

The planet is a whole within the larger whole of the solar system. You are a whole on the planet Earth. You, the Earth, and the solar system are all in motion. Movement is always seeking balance within a whole. Now is a time when your own action can help balance the Earth as a whole. This may be through an ecological action, planting a garden, trees, or flowers. Or it may be through pure consciousness as you embrace sentient beings on Earth. Your love of the Earth needs to be expressed at this time. You might paint a picture, write a poem or article about the Earth. Tune in to how you really feel about the planet. Is there sorrow about any devastation? Joy at her beauty? How might you go about balancing what is wounded to conform to a vision of greater reality you have? Now feel the elements in your body and realize how your body is made of the Earth. Feel at one with the planet.

COMPRESS AND EXPAND

Visualize and feel the essence of the Planet within your being. You and the Planet are made of the same stuff and can unfold your purpose together. Planet says, "Compress and congeal. Feel your beloved mother. Embrace the whole earth with your consciousness."

Affirmation:
I feel the qualities of the Earth in my body and our oneness heals us both.

84 Radiance

Now that you feel one with the Earth, you can express her radiance through your own wholehearted living. Your own heart and the radiance of the Earth are resonance. The Earth's radiance is in flowers, crystals, and the play of animals. Your's is in the expression of the Love-Light when you feel gratitude for your life, and the gifts of the Earth and sun. The more you radiate, the more you can feel that light is the circulation system of the whole universe. Your receptivity to the Love-Light can be opened through conscious breathing. Lie in the sun with eyes closed and breathe in light. The light you breathe in will be mixed with love and prana in your heart and the Love-Light you breathe out brings more radiance to the planet. Receive, be nourished, and grateful. Then express all that you love. The more you express love, the more you will radiate.

RADIATE LOVE

Visualize and feel Radiance as the yielding of awareness to the purity of color. Radiance says, "Shimmer and move. Love, laugh, and breathe light. You yourself are vibrations of color. Change stagnation on the planet to loving radiance."

Affirmation:
I breathe in the light of the sun, love of the Earth, and I radiate love and light.

46 Elements

You need to work with the Earth. Go to the beach, mountains, or your own back yard and commune with the elements. You may consider the elements of fire, air, water, and earth or the atomic elements of silica, copper and carbon, for example. Consider that your body, as well as the "bodies" of the Earth, sun, and stars, are made of these elements. Minerals, plants, and animals—in varying degrees, all share the same elements. Pay attention to the smallest details of a given project—your health, or work of art. Exact colors, shapes, and sounds are also elements. All elements have one thing in common: they are harmonious in varying degrees with each other. Some elements explode when combined, others bond, and yet others vibrate in resonance with each other. How do you relate to others through your elemental quality?

SEPARATE, DISSOLVE AND MIX

Visualize and feel the Elements within and all around you. Elements say, "Feel the fire, air, earth, and water meet and mix within you. Let the fluids flow and the gases intermingle. Feel the nourishment of the elements within you and supporting you."

Affirmation:

I appreciate the distinct qualites of elements and work with them to regenerate myself and all of life.

83 Seeing

Now you can see more clearly and with greater intensity as well as perspective. As you give and receive the Love-Light more and more you will be able to see how to use energy for the benefit of all. You may see how to use solar, wind, or water power to circulate energy from place to place. This implies seeing that people, nations, or continents are not separate from each other. All beings benefit when domineering control or manipulation is completely released. See how light, electromagnetic energy, and joy flow freely, and you will know that others see also. To see is to realize that all benefit when the energy circulates throughout the whole. You can see this, but can you take action on it? Is there something you can do to stimulate others to see, so that the Love-Light currency flows?

SEE AND FLOW

Visualize Seeing as the opening of the doors of your perception. Seeing says, "Behold the light shining in the darkness. Feel the spirit within all things transmuting pollution, toxicity, and blindness to the freeflow of light. As you change your perception you can change the world."

Affirmation:
I see how all of life is interconnected and that Love-Light is the currency and circulation system of the universe.

47 Growth

Your life is unfolding in a sequential manner that resonates with all of life. This is an evolutionary growth—gradual, step by step. Be patient and trust the process you are in. Don't attempt to get ahead of yourself. You can also appreciate the growth of other people, plants, and animals at this time. Tune into your body and realize that nature works very well. Talk to your cells and realize they can understand your intent. If you have the cooperation of your body and subconscious mind, your growth will unfold more easily, joyously, and with a deep sense of relaxation. Growth is happening in matter and mind at once. Your progressive development is assured if you live each moment at a time. Don't hesitate to grow into an unknown and uncertain space, even if you feel sensitive and vulnerable, like a tendril of a plant.

GROUND, SPROUT AND UNFURL

Visualize and feel Growth within and all around you. Growth says, "Receive sunlight, air, water, and food and be grateful to the source of all growth. Transform inactivity to an unfoldment of your purpose. Feel the combined elements being processed in new direction of growth."

Affirmation:
Step by step, my life is unfolding with a relaxed state of trust in each moment.

82 Rebirth

You are an agent of the rebirth of the planet through yourself. To fully realize this is to know eternity in every flower, star, and tree. In other words, you can now experience your own body and cells through the eternal Love-Light that knows the Oneness of your body as well as all other bodies. Rebirth can be painful or not, depending on your capacity to release the idea that everything unfolds slowly and sequentially. Rebirth is a sudden shift of awareness from the temporal to the eternal. Let the Love-Light permeate your being through the 'pores' of your cell's membranes. This is an adventure into the unknown. You are unique and, at once, universal. Let yourself go beyond time into a new creation. When you allow it, others will follow and the planet can be reborn.

ENERGIZE UNFOLDMENT

Visualize and feel Rebirth as a radiant womb of the heart, channeling light to sacred sites around the Earth. Rebirth says, "Energize unfoldment and emerge from dark confinement. Revitalize your soul."

Affirmation:
I am being reborn into my eternal being and I live in surprise, creating from the unknown.

48 Consciousness

Your consciousness may be on automatic. Now it is time to voluntarily use it to penetrate and understand other beings. Through consciousness, life reaches into intelligence through itself. Examine the patterns of life—the colors, forms, sounds, and gestures—keeping in mind that everything is mirrored in yourself as an unfoldment of evolution. You may be unconscious of a certain part of a problem you are in or are exploring. Allow yourself to have unfocused attention, as if staring at a blank wall. Allow your mind to simply be open. Sustain this open mind—without an object—for as long as you can. Now, what comes into your consciousness? Don't judge, censor, or let your mind wonder why. Just witness consciousness.

BE CONSCIOUS OF OTHERS THROUGH YOURSELF

Visualize and feel Consciousness within your mind, heart, and whole body. Consciousness says, "Behold others through yourself. Change unconscious ignorance to an awareness that the whole universe is alive and conscious. Feel all of evolution as your ancestral lineage."

Affirmation:
Through consciousness I participate in universal intelligence.

81 Illumination

Illumination is a choice to purify enough to see that there are neither separations in nature nor in spirit. Each photon contains all other photons, but in illumination they are radiated out as suns and stars within the human mind. Give your attention to everything you see, realizing everything is an undivided wholeness. And this wholeness is made up only of Love-Light. Nothing else. Feel, open and behold the Love-Light until you *become* it and are fully illumined yourself. This implies a release of tensions, strife, and struggle. Allow your consciousness to be vigilant but relaxed, trusting the Oneness. At the moment you fully trust the Oneness, you are illuminated. You can choose to be whole.

ENLIGHTEN

Visualize and feel Illumination as the inner light of consciousness, centered in your heart. Illumination says, "Shine within. Remember, you are one with the source of the sun. Change opacity to transparency and burn through obstructions with the fire of consciousness."

Affirmation:
I become the Love-Light by seeing the blessed truth and wholeness of everything I see.

49 Cosmic Law

You can now bring through and execute something that is truly founded on the laws of the universe. Don't hesitate to stand firm in what you have intuitively seen and chosen to do. If you are uncertain, evaluate what you have done in the past. Sift the wheat from the chaff of your values until you find some principles that have worked for you. Question yourself: Is it regenerative? That is, does it lead to some new beginning like seeds from fruit? Is it holographic? Is its pattern found in many places in the universe? Is it hierarchical? Is there a priority of values? Is it transcendent? Does the law point beyond itself into the unknown? These may be some criteria for evaluating the principle to find, the law to live. Now open again to the universal law that you need for the next step in your unfoldment.

FIND UNIVERSAL CONSTANTS

Visualize and feel Cosmic Law permeating your being. Cosmic Law says, "Find universal constants. Discover wholeness and what applies in many cases. Release what is random and question your own motives and values.
What is your criterion for truth?"

Affirmation:
I am basing my values on the deepest cosmic laws I am aware of.

80 Truth

You can now dare to *live* your truth. Have the courage to live your sovereignty fully now. All that has been illusion or falsehood in your life is being consumed. How so? By a release of rigid views and emotional attachments. Pray for the truth only. Each moment you ask for truth and open to it unconditionally, you live it more. If you wonder whether something is true or not, embody it. Don't try to figure it out. The little mind never can. Truth is state of being, not knowledge. It is found and lived by removing all obscurations, resistances to living who you are. Truth is the highest rate of vibration of a thought-field in harmony with your deep presence. Relax while being aware. The Love-Light flows into every moment you live truth.

EMBODY TRUTH

Visualize and feel Truth as the manifestation of spirit within you. Truth says, "Your life is the way. Change outworn laws and rules to the living truth. Changed fixed views to spontaneous action. Trust your discernment."

Affirmation:
I am living the truth of my being.

50 Self-Conflict

Are you dividing your desires from the wholeness of your being? One way to change self-conflict is to intensify it while witnessing it until it dissolves into a state of peace. Another way is to avoid it, in which case it will intensify by itself. In either case it is well to realize that it has a purpose—to impress your consciousness with the fact that you are judging to a point of extreme tension. This tension comes from more than a conflict of values. It is a conflict of a part of yourself with the whole of yourself. The part can create tension and resistance, but only the whole can find peace. Let go of any separation, especially self-centered attachments and release blaming yourself. Breathe deeply and embrace the conflict. See what happens.

SEPARATE FROM COSMIC LAW

Visualize and feel Self-Conflict within you as a reflection of the values of the world. Self-Conflict says, "Separate one thing from another and polarize extremes. Change unity to diversity and allow conflict to emerge. Only by dynamic confrontation can you begin to see your blind spots. See what values your ancestors and culture imposed on you."

Affirmation:
I am breathing deeply and releasing all judgement.

79 Passage

You can now go through any obstacles, for you are embodying the truth. You are transparent to blocks you had before. Or if not, you are about to be. Ask for the truth only. Pray to be guided by truth. Listen and open you heart and mind to what is right. This has nothing to do with custom, habit, traditional law, morality, or what others may think. Passage is the ongoing quality of your life when you are guided by truth each moment. You can't know ahead of time what each moment's truth will be. Your awareness will open to knowing with the heart and mind simultaneous with your action. Your feelings, thoughts, and deeds are now in total oneness with the Love-Light carrying you through the most difficult times.

PASS THROUGH

Visualize and feel Passage as the entry and passage of living truth. Passage says, "Release old habits and move on. Be one with truth and move through resistance. Change judgement to awakened response and self-conflict to creative challenge."

Affirmation:
I pass through difficulties by maintaining a oneness
of heart, mind, and action.

51 Trials

It may seem as if you are tossed in turbulent waves, or against an impossible adversary, but this is all a quest to discover truth within yourself. Ask yourself: How can I regenerate or bring forth my greatest worth? How can I express the source of truth in myself? These are questions of self-esteem and confidence. You have trials wherever there are fears. And these fears originate in wounds in your heart, soul, mind, and body. These wounds are now stored in your cellular memory. Cease blaming yourself and simply feel. Face your opponent and embrace her, him, or it. Let the trials be a process of dispelling traumas. Cease being attached to the outcome and focus on how you feel—while holding a space for the trials. This is a test of faith in yourself and trust in the divine.

STRUGGLE, LONG AND TRY

Visualize and feel Trials as the impulses that want to discern truth from falsehood. Trials say, "Struggle, battle, and try. Change complacency and apathy into an effort to find out how things work. Try many things and face the unknown. What is at the root of your own trials?"

Affirmation:
I accept trials as a test of faith when I stand up for what I value.

78 Opening

Now that you have gone through the fires you can open to a new life. You may feel you are being pulled into a tsunami wave or whirlwind, but this is the moment of opening to truth. Timing is important in entry. Energy is flowing and you've come to the critical edge of the wave. Be constant in your intent to enter and go through. All trials are transformed in this moment of opening. Open your heart and mind to the Oneness of life. Embrace adversity if it comes to you, for you are large enough to hold difficulty in the Love-Light until it melts. Opening is an energy change from limited perspective and course of action to an all-embracing circle of possibilities. Now you can choose your life values. Your new life is beginning with unforeseen doorways appearing before you.

OPEN YOUR HEART AND EMBRACE

Visualize and feel Opening as a doorway to truth that enables you to let go of denial. Opening says, "Come in and cross over. Change blocks, trials and tribulations to a simple opening of new pathways. Stay on the edge of the vivid unknown."

Affirmation:
I am opening to more and more opportunities
and am constant in my intention.

52 Conscience

You are now evaluating what is good and what is evil in your own thoughts, words, and deeds. To examine yourself in this way is beneficial, but you need to know what your criteria for good and evil are. Is it based on cultural values, the morality of your parents? All faiths have much the same universal morality (do not kill, lie, steal etc.). Whatever faith or tradition you belong to or are influenced by, discern whether you are blaming yourself unduly or not seeing where you really have erred. Simply be aware of mistakes and correct them. There is no need for guilt. Guilt is merely an excuse for not making correction! Acknowledge your errors and make a clear dedication in thought, word, and deed to make correction. Then your conscience will be clear.

SEE THE RIGHTNESS OF UNITY

Visualize Conscience as the truth of values in relation to cosmic law and the world. Conscience says, "You can't get away with anything. See unity and rightness in the midst of diversity and confusion. Examine what you deny and face the consequences of your actions. Be honest with yourself and stand up for your truth regardless of the status quo."

Affirmation:
I know the source of my code of ethics and I correct mistakes without blame.

77 *Confession*

To confess where you have gone wrong releases obstructions to your actually making corrections in your life. Confession is the beginning of knowing wholeness through the living Love-Light. Knowing wholeness corrects the part that resists wholeness, and enables you to contribute to the culture as a whole. This is an ego-dissolving process—where you see the whole of yourself, of culture, of humanity as interconnected through truth. When you confess to yourself any errors, you are liberated by truth. This enables you to see your part in relation to culture, humanity, and the universe as a whole. Sometimes it may imply a complete surrender of any self-centered position to benefit the whole group. The deeper your confession—without blaming yourself—the more clear and whole you are and the more you embody truth.

GO WITH THE TRUTH

Visualize and feel Confession as an open, all-accepting honesty. Confession says, "Ask for truth and dissolve all falsehood. Change denial and defensiveness to open confessions. Realize how, in the past, you may have projected blame, but now are resolved to accept your own errors."

Affirmation:
I confess mistakes I've made in the past and take action on my rightful calling.

53 Healing

You need to slow down, stop, and go within for a time. Allow your compassionate witness to reflect on how your body feels. Listen to your cells. They want to be acknowledged and appreciated for serving you so well, so long. Healing is not only physical, but is an integration of body, psyche, and spirit. This is not possible unless you cease driving yourself. Listen to your spirit. Attune soul and mind to spirit and your body will rest and renew. If you are coming down with, or recovering from some illness, reflect on what emotional desires and fears contributed to it. See how your thought-forms may have been driven in circles by these emotions. Let go of control. Surrender to the divine Love-Light that heals all. Realize you are loved.

GO WITHIN AND SURRENDER TO GOD

Visualize and feel Healing as a sphere around you that is filled with transformative subtle essences. Healing says, "Go within and accept your vulnerability. Change any old defensiveness to an open sense of being. Transform your fear of pain into an experience of balanced sensitivity. Now experience vulnerability as tenderness."

Affirmation:
I am loved and am listening to my body and soul,
and I cease all addictive tendencies.

76 Marriage

The masculine and feminine aspects of yourself are now capable of true inner marriage. When this is fulfilled, your chance of fulfillment in a balanced relationship is much greater than before. Marriage is a profound realization of the flow of the Love-Light through every fibre of your being. All the frustrations you may have had in the past—about uniting with the opposite sex—can now be transformed by a simple embrace and acceptance of your overreaction to your mother and father. Embrace any conflicts with love. Be aware that conflicts and frustrations are but energy trapped in fragmented thought-forms. They will transmute when you are ready to let the Love-Light flow through your being. Then the body ravishes in purity the partner it has chosen.

JOIN AND FULFILL

Visualize and feel Marriage as the fusion of opposites within you. Marriage says, "Acknowledge differences and see how they work together. Allow the fusion of the masculine and feminine within you. Melt, open, and be fulfilled. Change separation and opposition to inner union."

Affirmation:
I am realizing how I have unconsciously reacted to my parents and am now balancing my inner masculine and feminine.

54 Awareness

Now that you are more integrated, your awareness is increasing. Trust your capacity to see multidimensionally and penetrate beyond appearances. Your challenge is to stay aware in all circumstances—whether pleasurable, neutral, or painful. You may even find that your awareness is present even during sleep. Don't be taken in by what people want you to see or think. Have faith that your awareness reaches behind masks and disguises. You may be in a difficult situation—even imprisoned—but your awareness can go beyond the walls if your attention persists in a steady intention of neutrality. Reactive emotion, such as anger or blame, will quickly diminish your awareness. Cultivate serenity and neutrality and your awareness will liberate you.

ATTENTION! SEE THE WAY OUT!

Visualize Awareness as an all encompassing power to be alert and vigilant. Awareness says, "See the way out and penetrate falsehood. Behold your own deceptions and illusions, and see them for what they are. Change distraction and dullness into clear attention."

Affirmation:
I am increasing my awareness of the Truth of what is happening.

75 Clarity

Now you can see clearly. You may have lied to yourself in the past—to avoid pain—but now you have such clarity that such deception is no longer possible. You need to be clear about yourself before you can be clear about anyone else. Purifying your life in any way—diet, exercise, aura cleansing—brings you greater clarity. Go within and examine any painful experiences and search for their roots in illusion or confusion. Were you misled? Why did you want to believe it? Were your ideals so inflated that you didn't see what was actually happening? Self-honesty is essential for clarity to shine in your being. You may need to go through painful memories. Some hidden desire or fear may be at the root of illusions you may have. Just look into the face of that desire or fear and anything illusory will pop like a bubble and your clarity will reveal itself.

BEHOLD WITH INTEGRITY

Visualize and feel Clarity as lucid intelligence within you. Clarity says, "Look into your beloved's eyes and see clearly. Do you see your beloved or the projection of what you want them to be? Change confusion and vagueness to a love that sees."

Affirmation:
Through self-honesty and purification I become more clear
by dispelling illusions.

55 Will

You need to use will now, but not in a struggling or stressful way. Use will as an extension of intention. Consistently pour into action the awareness you have. You may be constantly making more clear your intention as you use will to stand up to adversity or overcome obstacles. The main thing is to get clear on what you are doing and persist in a direction that is for the highest good for everyone involved. Will can easily become control and manipulation, either of yourself or others. This is detrimental, for the right use of will is a love-will deep in the soul, and is not domineering at all. However there are cases where someone being destructive needs to be stopped, and the best way to do this is not by force, but by consistent positive action in accordance with clear intention. The negative will then fall of its own accord. You can do this now.

MOVE IN THE INTENDED DIRECTION

Visualize and feel Will as your ability to move, create, endure, and sustain what you chose. Will says, "Initiate your true vision. Move in a direction. Change uncertainty and hesitation into a power that will manifest what you see as true."

Affirmation:
I use my will with a clear intent for the benefit of everyone concerned.

74 Power

Your power is through the presence of your higher self. Power is neither rigid nor stubborn, but is nevertheless firm in its truth. Power initiates flexibility through forgiveness. Open yourself to the divine Love-Light within you and you will receive an empowerment. Your sovereignty is here involved. If you have a tendency to give your power away, or to be involved in power struggles, you are not being receptive enough to the Love-Light coming through your higher self. If that is the case, stop, cease any effort, and open yourself to the divine presence. Listen. Be receptive. The power may come as an increase of subtle energy, as light, or a clear sense of direction. When it comes, allow it to reveal its power. This is a turning of the wheel of the law, sometimes symbolized as a swastika. This is not a negative symbol, but one that has been abused.

TURN THE WHEEL OF THE LAW

Visualize and feel Power as an inner strength flowing from the source which vitalizes your entire being. Power says, "Turn the cosmic wheel. Change rigidity to firmness and self-will to empowerment. Your power is not a force or domination, but a presence."

Affirmation:
I receive power from the divine Love-Light and use it for the enlightenment of myself and others.

56 Integration

Your soul, body, and mind are coming into a greater integration with your spirit. The many levels of your being are becoming purified and amalgamated to discover your eternal adamantine self. If you feel you are being pulled in various directions, this is an indication that there is resistance to becoming integrated. Thought and feeling are deeply linked in your cellular memory. If there is a trauma or old hurt (conscious or unconscious) that still holds negative thought-forms, it is essential to give your attention to any painful sensations you may feel in your body. Go into the pain and allow images to come forth if they will. Maintain awareness and continue to let go of reacting during intense feeling. Do this for as long as needed and you will naturally become integrated.

CENTER ALL CHANGE

Visualize and feel Integration as a plenitude of the many aspects of yourself. Integration ways, "See the unity in diversity. Change separation, fragmentation, and self-alienation to inclusiveness and holism.
Feel all aspects of yourself as one whole."

Affirmation:
By consistent awareness and centering, I allow all aspects of myself to become integrated.

73 *Androgyne*

Inwardly, on a subtle level, you are both male and female. Androgyne is the alchemical marriage within. Embrace all opposites within yourself and experience polarities as a fusion of your male and female psychospiritual energy. If you acknowledge ancient wounds and work through a fusion of opposites within, you to create a vibrational matrix for revealing the Androgyne within. You are now in a state where you can completely cease projecting on your partner—your ideals for the opposite sex. It is imperative to actually listen, look, and be open to who they are in and of themselves. This is one test for you to realize how complete the Androgyne (male and female fusion) is in you. You will feel the Love-Light when the Androgyne is being fulfilled.

FIND WHOLENESS WITHIN

Visualize and feel Androgyne as the balance of the masculine and feminine within your soul. Androgyne says, "Look at and feel the complements of your animus (male) or your anima (female) within. What qualities complement and which ones oppose? How can you work with these tensions?"

Affirmation:
I acknowledge projections and realize the balance of my own masculine and feminine within.

57 Generation

You can now generate what you need for your family, friends, and society as a whole. Generation is your capacity to open to the vital force and the energies of the universe, and draw them forth toward a synthesis that benefits culture. This includes powerful sexuality and spiritual presence. Don't hesitate to go forth to do what you feel needs to be done. The purity and power of your feelings are the guides for this evolutionary and cultural change. This is a personal empowerment that can impel the right change in family, professional, or societal structures. Trust the inrush of energy and allow it to work through yourself and everyone involved. You can take initiative and succeed in bringing forth a more vital and loving order in your group. Realize your own leadership.

GENERATE SUCCESSION

Visualize and feel Generation as your power to bring a purposeful succession to your family or group. Generation says, "Be yourself. Give of your seed, property and blood to your children and successors. Change impotency to potency and the power of lineage and tradition."

Affirmation:
I am taking initiative in generating social changes needed in my community or group.

72 Synarchy

Now that you are confident of your own empowerment, you can work with others in a council process. Remember that each person is sovereign in and of themselves—which enables each to contribute to the whole in a synergistic way. Your own contribution is natural and easy for you to give and is very needed by the group as a whole. Realize that only *you* have the unique gifts that you have. And this also is true with each person. Any competitiveness is completely out of place in Synarchy. If competetiveness comes up, consider it a transformation process towards Synarchy. Simply be aware of how it feels and continue to relate to others in an open, honest way. When you meditate, pray, work, or discuss with others, be aware of the gift of presence of each person. If gratitude wells up in your heart, you are truly part of Synarchy.

HONOR EACH WITHIN THE WHOLE

Visualize and feel Synarchy as a group consciousness within your being and your relationship to other people. Synarchy says, "Include and fulfill. Change separatist goals into harmonious attunement. Accept each unique person and being as a creative gift for the collective."

Affirmation:
I feel so confident in my unique gifts that I can honor and receive those of others.

58 Uniformity

You are now in the repetitive routine of life, and need to accept this as a practise for a while. It is only by total acceptance of the situation that you will become free of painful pressure. Uniformity is a way of social alignment that entrains the nervous system to be in a daily rhythm with others. There are adjustments to be made so that the group works as a whole and moves more smoothly. Strong individuality is out of place now. On the other hand, you, as an individual, can learn greater humility and respect for others, and can even compete with others now. This does not mean you identify with what you do. Let go of identity and enjoy the common rhythms of life.

ORGANIZE RHYTHMS

Visualize and feel Uniformity as the status quo, the repetition and competition of life. Uniformity says, "Change erratic behavior into routines. Discover the oscillation of work, play, and sleep. Stay in the rhythms and values of the mundane world."

Affirmation:
I work with others in daily rhythms of life that need regulation to fulfill a purpose.

71 Technology

Being confident in yourself and clear in your relation with others, you can use technology—whether simple like a fork, or complex like a computer—to fulfill your contribution to the common good. Technology is a means, not an end. Use it wisely as a means to fulfill your soul purpose. Cultural technology is a conscious enactment of how wholes interact with wholes. Your body has a very delicate, complex, and orderly technology. Realize how you can contribute to the cultural body by using technology. The main thing is to ask: for what purpose or greater end is technology used? Then consider what is the best technology to use in a given case. It might be simple or complex, mimic nature, or be an invention unseen before. By all means do it with love.

INVENT AND DESIGN

Visualize and feel Technology as an extension of your mind, limbs, and senses into the world. Technology says, "Understand nature's inner-directed technologies. Find delicate means to embrace and modulate how nature works within you and within her kingdoms. Tools can be refined and made precise, in harmony with nature's rhythms and spirits."

Affirmation:
I use tools as a means to express my love for my community or group.

59 Revolution

Accept that there are great reversals and cycles now in your life. It is time for experiencing the sides of life you may have ignored or denied in the past. Let go of all judgements about what is happening, for they only accentuate any "problems." Just experience the changes with awareness. Go ahead and be radical now—your energy and insights can offer a possible breakthrough in your social milieux. Realize there is no going back to the way things were. Go on to the inspiration of new relationships or new ways of relating to old relationships. Go on and apply your energies to social ideas that bring change to the status quo. Get perspective on how you have been conditioned by your parents and your culture. Your personality is undergoing a radical revolution by shaking loose old habits. Trust your deep self to come through the revolution.

BE RADICAL AND SHIFT POSITIONS

Visualize and feel Revolution as the power to overturn despotic or tyrannical rule. Revolution says, "Be radical when necessary. Change temperance, compromise, and patience into outright revolution. There is no going back now.
Go forth and transform."

Affirmation:
The change in my relationships is a part of a great social transition.

70 Cooperation

Now that your individuality is established in the Love-Light you can work with others in a totally cooperative way. If you have any fear of being dominated, or of competition remaining, you can trust that it will be dispelled. Your relationships will be strengthened by your listening to and acknowledging the gifts and contributions of others in your social group, family, or working team. You can be a tremendously positive force now simply by your presence and awareness. Place less emphasis on *doing* anything and more on being simply aware. A more whole, synergistically harmonious group is arising in your midst. The more you recognize others around you who are capable of true cooperation the more the new culture will emerge. Let go of dependency in this cooperation. Cooperation is interdependency. Open to the wonder and ease of it.

LISTEN AND COOPERATE WITH OTHERS

Visualize and feel Cooperation as an agreement between yourself and others. Cooperation says, "Hold and act in common, for you are one whole. Change competition and uncertainty to cooperation and your returns will be multiplied a hundredfold."

Affirmation:
I cooperate with other people by realizing my own individuality as well as the value of others.

125

60 Regeneration

It is wonderful that you are including as many types of people as you can in a regenerative process you are involved in. Your body, soul and/or mind are regenerative by including others in your prayers and thoughts. At times you may feel uncertain of your orientation in relation to others, but this can be remedied by going deeply into your center—in your heart and solar plexus—and including the very people or situations that make you apprehensive. The way of regeneration is by reaching out to others in all directions, and though you don't know what will come of it, trust that seeds of new beginnings are in the fruit of your growth. Seek not the fruit, but simply stay centered while reaching out. Like a tree your group will regenerate.

FIND SOURCE AND REGENERATE

Visualize and feel Regeneration as the power to include other races, cultures, and ways of being in your life. Regeneration says, "Be resourceful and all-inclusive. Exclude no one from your heart and meet the challenges of difference. Change discrimination and exclusiveness to finding a place for each and all."

Affirmation:
I reach out to others of diverse types and trust the greater process of the oneness of humanity.

69 Individuality

Now that you are more fully accepting of yourself, you can give of yourself to others. Let the Love-Light shine through and allow yourself to be responsive to other's needs. You can initiate what you see as needed in any given situation. Your individuation is feeling a wholeness of body, soul, mind, and spirit so that all struggle ceases. This means your conditioned personality has been or is being shorn of its relative fearful or domineering aspects. It means your higher self and ego have come to terms and are at peace with each other. You cannot kill your ego (or it will kill you!) but you *can* allow it a place of governing the practical mind and feelings, which in turn are receptive to the directives of the higher mind and spiritual body. Your individuality is a wonderful wholeness and peacefulness. Enjoy!

BE EMPOWERED AS YOURSELF

Visualize and feel Individuality as a specific force that runs through your unique being. Individuality says, "Be unto yourself. Change insecurity to self-acceptance. Accept the whole within yourself and yourself within the whole."

Affirmation:
I acknowledge my unique individuality as a wholeness to offer to the greater whole society.

61 Ecstasy

As you break out of the illusory world projection, ecstasy will fill your being. When you love God you will experience an ecstatic liberation. Purify your mind, heart and body. Allow the Love-Light to shine through your cells. Realize that this bliss takes incessant practise with the intent of liberation from illusion for all beings. Often pain is part of the process of releasing obstructions to the ecstasy. Let the bliss come, but don't try to control it or cling to it. Pain and ecstasy may well alternate as you continue to peel away layers of aeons of defensiveness. Just know that for ecstasy, there is only one way to go: on and on, dispelling illusions, living through pain, and letting it all go. Ecstasy is your path to freedom.

BREAK OUT OF THE PROGRAM

Visualize and feel Ecstasy as a whirling light within your heart, expanding your being. Ecstasy says, "Purify yourself in diet, thoughts, and feelings and you will feel bliss. Feel oneness with all things. Change limitation and confusion to ecstatic radiance. Feel the conception of your divine self from purification."

Affirmation:
*I become more ecstatic the more I surrender to the Love-Light
and dispel illusion.*

68 Purity

You can now actualize your pure vision and feeling of how life can be. Purity fulfills giving. As you give in purity, you are receptive to the gifts of heaven. Seek no rewards for your thoughts, words, or deeds, but let the purity be a divine gift of the Love-Light. Purity is the pristine fulfillment of the Celestial Earth within you. Purity is the experience of simultaneous suffering and bliss. Let your intention rise beyond the realms of effects. Seek no results except the purity of each instant. Moment by moment, you can accept whatever is happening to you or around you. Live for the good of all—even your "enemies." This purity is not an idea nor ideal, but a living experience of acceptance and peace amidst either adversity or bliss. Wonder of wonders! You live now in purity!

PURIFY AND ACTUALIZE

Visualize and feel Purity within your body, mind, and heart. Purity says, "Live each moment and be attentive. Release all habits that do not reveal your essence. Change conflicted, mixed thoughts to open wonder and pure delight."

Affirmation:
I seek no rewards but give with a pure intention to trusting the fulfillment of the whole.

62 Creativity

The ecstasy within you is pouring out in new patterns that open your creative potential. Creativity takes you far beyond the ego as you allow inspiration to move within you towards courageous action. You can now go through your fears of not being accepted or loved. You can move in a realm of pure creative joy. Sometimes pain may be experienced if parts of yourself resist the flow of divine consciousness through you. Let the pain be and let it change. Creativity is a flux that can actualize new ways of life as well as works of art or invention. Sing, dance, use color, and allow your inner child a place to play and unfold. Nothing is inevitable, but is open to creative possibilities.

CREATE EVER NEW PATTERNS

Visualize and feel Creativity as the interconnecting matrix of the divine womb of the cosmic mother all around you. Creativity says, "Fill the matrix with love and abundance will spring from you. Change confinement to an outpouring of ecstasy in ever new patterns. Meet the challenges of life with resourcefulness. Let the new be conceived within you."

Affirmation:
I participate in the creative flow and enjoy the spontaneous innovation from within myself.

67 Construction

You are now so consistently creative that you can be a conscious culture-maker in the Celestial Earth. This construction is a step by step action inspired through a utopian vision which is actually a deep memory of a pure and pristine Earth. Heavenly rest is intrinsic to Earth activity when you construct out of the Love-Light. Wholeness is inherent in all things and as you draw this wholeness out, a new culture is constructed. Be receptive first, then being moved by what inspires you, allow yourself to take action consistently. Day by day, moment by moment, move in a direction of construction. Let destruction go. The outworn will destroy itself in time. Your purpose is unfolding out of a trust in wholeness within each and every being. Explore designs, possible forms for building, relationships, business or any aspect of life that interests you.

CONSISTENTLY CREATE

Visualize and feel Construction as the power to manifest inspired design through daily action. Construction says, "Design and build. Change random movements to progressive steps in creating a Celestial Earth. Be guided by the joy and beauty of your purpose in what you construct."

Affirmation:
I am consistently manifesting the vision of my greatest values.

63 Service

You can give of yourself freely now, even though you still feel you are separate from others. Memory is the code of life possibilities which are recreated as service to life. As you remember more clearly your true purpose you will know what your possibilities are. Be happy to serve others—especially those in quest of the divine. But realize that even the beggar, the criminal, the confused—are all on a quest for the divine beloved. Your presence, given with love, is a sign to them, of the divine beloved. Have faith that service, with a good intent, delivers you also to the next station closer to the divine. In all benevolent thoughts, words, and action you are brought closer to the source, the Creator. When you see others as yourself and care for them as you would yourself, you are truly serving with devotion.

SERVE THE CREATOR

Visualize and feel Service as the birth of yourself into the world. Service says, "I and thou art one, yet I long to give and receive. I receive the gift of life and want to serve life. By accepting myself into the here and now, I can help others."

Affirmation:
I am serving my fellow human and sentient beings with simple responsiveness.

66 Devotion

Now you realize you are one with the divine beloved—the object of your devotion. There is no separation between you and what or who you serve. Devotion reveals the mutually arising Oneness between self and other. In a spirit of devotion with open heart, you can perform any action—however attractive or irksome it may be—with equanimity. With devotion you die to likes and dislikes and are reborn to the meaning of life. Dead memory becomes poetry when you trust your devoted heart. This poetry is the full expression of your self-acceptance. Devote yourself to music, art, gardening, cleaning the kitchen, or opening a business. The more fully you devote yourself to a task, the more peace and love you will experience. The Love-Light will flood your being as you express devotion. Devotion itself is an attitude that unites all polarities.

UNITE WITH YOUR BELOVED

Visualize and feel Devotion as a feeling of oneness with your work, lover, teacher, or child. Devotion says, "Change contention and separation into mutual activity. Meet yourself through others and devote yourself to the One in each and all."

Affirmation:
I am devoted to my work, friends, tasks, and God in equal measure—for we are one.

64 Freedom

Your freedom is not a freedom from others, the world or reality, but is a freedom from attachment. Detachment is an unfurling of the petals of liberation. The less you identify with specific thoughts, feelings or ideals, the more free you will be. All your life you have been in a cage of conditions, entrained and bred into you. Now you can begin to release these conditions and realize that your true being cannot be possessed. Freedom is a kind of sacrifice—in so far as you see both good and evil as sacred, as part of the whole. When you go deep enough, there is no clinging and nothing can imprison you in this state of pure freedom. Be who you are and you are free!

RELEASE AND RETURN TO SOURCE

Visualize and feel Freedom as lotus petals of fulfillment of your creative life. Freedom says, "Release all possessiveness and move on. Enjoy the variety of life. Change attachment and clinging to flexibility and delightful uncertainty. With confidence, live in each moment."

Affirmation:
I become more free the more I release conditioning that is not for my highest good.

65 Giving

Realizing your oneness with all of life—good and evil—you know that in giving to 'others' there can be no loss nor gain. Giving is the fundamental quality that is to spread throughout the New Earth. The Love-Light shines through every act of Giving. The rays of Love-Light reach the true being in freedom, and it is returned with interest in Giving. Give away what you don't use. Pass on what riches come to you—whether in money, goods, or wisdom and love. Giving to those in need expands the essence of all one has received and returns it to the whole. The expansion of giving brings forth illumination and insight so that a conscious offering to the divine beloved is fulfilled.

GIVE AND RECEIVE THROUGH ALL THINGS

Visualize and feel Giving flooding you as an expression of a free state of being. Giving says, "Give thanks and give offerings. You receive through everything you meet. Change lack and impoverishment to gratitude, and abundance will flow forth."

Affirmation:
I give freely and let God judge right and wrong—for I know the oneness of life.

What Paths are You Walking?

To see a larger pattern of how various cards you pick are related to each other, you can chart your Medicine Paths. These paths reveal a mythopoetic and yet practical guide of awareness. Like the *Vibrational Healing Cards* and readings themselves, they are a mirror. They reflect who you are, where you've come from, and your direction for the future. The difference is that with the Medicine Paths you get a larger perspective on your life through the use of groups of cards.

Proceedure

Make several photocopies, enlarged if you wish, of both the New Earth and Old Earth Charts. You will use these copies to circle the symbols of the *Vibrational Healing Cards* over a period of time, or in relation to a given series of questions. It will be helpful to number the *time* order of your questions and corresponding symbols so that you know which *Vibrational Healing Cards* correspond with which questions. As you pick more cards and circle their corresponding symbols, notice whether they are on a vertical, horizontal or diagonal axis. Then look up the pattern in the charts of the Medicine Paths on the following eight pages. Look up the corresponding reading on pages 145 to 168.

Old Earth Path Readings are from pages 145 to 157. The order of the Paths is from Horizontal, to Existence, to Essence, to Vertical. New Earth Paths are from pages 157 to 169 and the order is reversed: Vertical, Essence, Existence to Horizontal. The names of the symbols on each end of the Path you are considering are the key to finding the right path. They are under the *name* of the Path in the Readings. Only the two symbols on the extreme ends of the Path are given under the name. For example, the horizontal Old Earth Path called *"Energizing Modules"*: 41 energy - 62 creativity includes the 42 mass, 45 planet, 46 elements, 57 generation, 58 uniformity, and 61 ecstasy as well.

The Medicine Planes between the Old Earth and New Earth are introduced on page 170.

Old Earth Horizontal Medicine Paths

Centering						
Light and Dark Pulsating Visions						
Cosmic Templating						
Interrelating and Networking						
Holographic Receptivity						
Working Through						
Energizing Modules						
Manifesting and Reciprocating						

Old Earth Essence Axis Medicine Paths

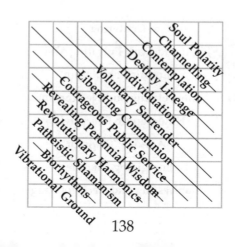

Old Earth Existence Axis Medicine Paths

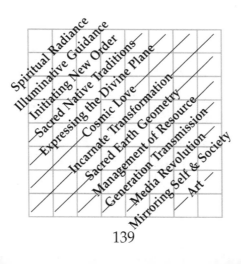

Old Earth Vertical Medicine Paths

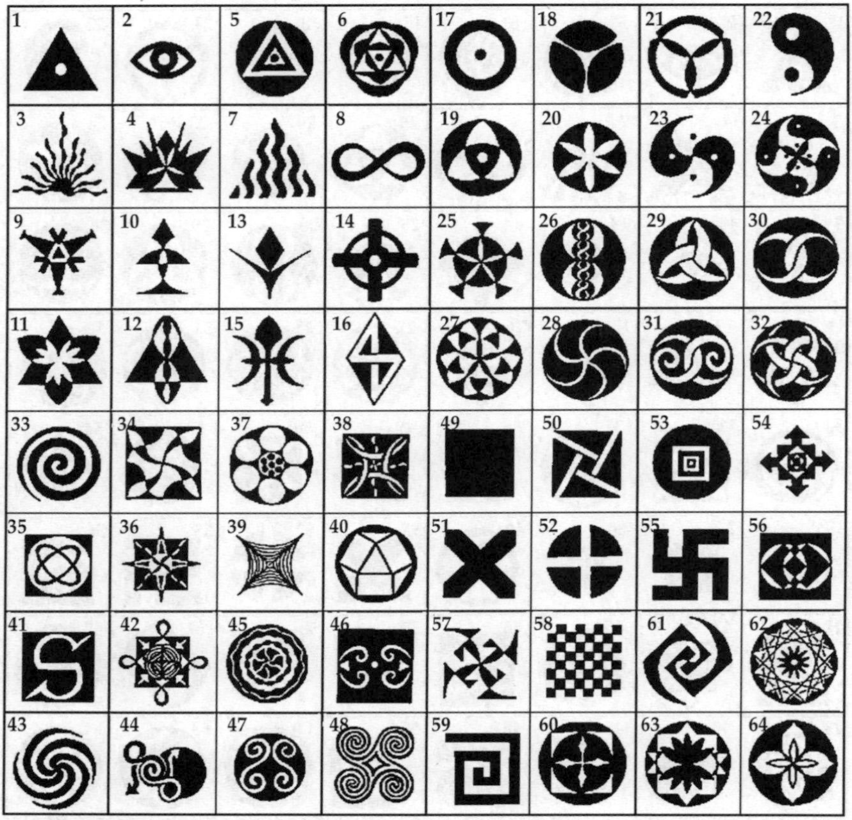

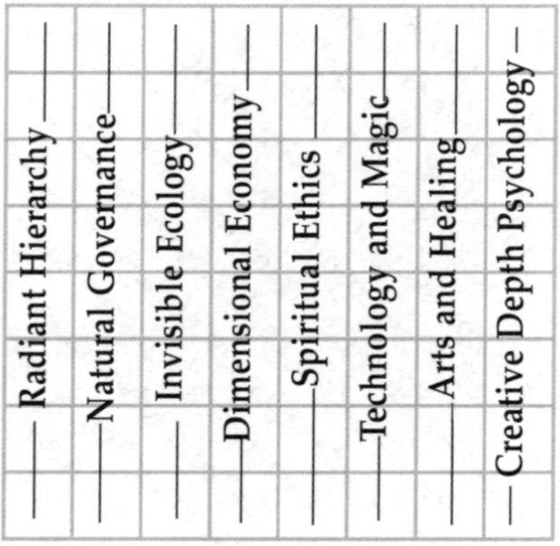

New Earth Vertical Medicine Paths

New Earth Existence Axis Medicine Paths

New Earth Essence Medicine Paths

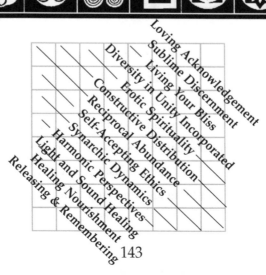

New Earth Horizontal Medicine Paths

	Spiritual Fulfillment	
	Transmutation	
	Global Networking	
	Trusting Your Poetry	
Ethical Clarity & Resonant Healing		
	Constancy Amidst Change	
Building and Communicating		
	Social Ecology	

OLD EARTH
Paths of the Old Earth Creative Process
(Horizontal)

1 Centering:
(1 Eternity - 22 Desire)

You can now initiate creativity at one with spiritual sources. You can act from the deep oneness you may feel when you are truly centered. Cherish eternal moments and know that they occur when you are most yourself. Keep love and desires in balance with your fullest spiritual intention and you will have vast potential for accessing resources. You may start a project which demands your utmost creativity now.

2 Light and Dark Pulsating Visions:
(3 Spiritual Fire - 24 Shadows)

This path can guide you to have glimpses of primal processes where everything is chaotic or turbulent. But even such primal processes have their own order which enables a restructuring of your life. By allowing the break down of old forms there will be an illumination of shadows and blind spots you have tried to hide in the past. Open your intuition and live in the expansion of your full auric field and you will be able to see new creative possibilities. You can now learn both the illness and the art of the power of projection. Release reactive hallucinated projections and clear visions will arise.

3 Cosmic Templating:
(9 Guidance - 30 Reason)

You can draw or make high order models of culture based on ancient wisdom. You can also see codes in fields of genetics, microbiology and physics. You might enter into fields of engineering and create models for computer systems. Have the courage of your convictions, for you can find formal patterns in any system that can provide a clear base for deeper understanding. Mathematics can be used to great advantage especially if you use imagination as well as reason. You can design blueprints for whatever is needed.

4 Interrelating and Networking:
(11 Order - 32 Thought)

You are now empowered in areas of communications and media of all kinds. As you examine ancient civilizations, you may find particular qualities that provided the transmission of certain codes, models and matrices which are applicable now. You can make new connections, not only in how systems work together, but in the minds of people. You might communicate about your discoveries in history, but also in physiology and mechanics. You can access patterns through memory, and as you express the harmonious and disharmonious paths of historic times, you can bring forth relevant information for the present time.

5 Holographic Receptivity:
(33 Vortex - 54 Awareness)

This path can guide you to an awareness of how the sources of nature and culture are the results of a projection of intent. You can then see yourself as a holographic image within the projection. Look at the universe as a model of wholes within wholes and see how seed-ideas become images, and how images work within dimensional laws. Be aware of ethical considerations when bringing your creative project down into detailed drawings and plans. Conflicts in any area of life can pollute the whole image. Rectify problems by being receptive to the holographic model.

6 Working Through:
(35 Time - 56 Integration)

Living in the time-space world of forms brings many trials, but these very difficulties are the key to turning self-will towards a more fully integrated self with love-will. Have the patience to work with the forms in nature. Observe how certain forms are universal and others specific. See how metamorphosis works in embryology. You can now harmonize nature and culture through the discovery of your own wholeness.

7 Energizing Modules:
(41 Energy - 62 Creativity)

This path guides you to make your ideas and plans tangible and to infuse them with energy. Working in fields of physics, geology or chemistry is relevant now for finding the right means to make tangible what you have created. You might combine elements into new patterns and duplicate them. Bring the traditions of the past into technological changes through communication, travel and the cataloguing of information. Above all, bring energy to projects and you will likely feel ecstatic.

8 Manifesting and Reciprocating:
(43 Inertia - 64 Freedom)

You are now fully conscious of the ground of tangible existence and can manifest the inventions you have been working on. You can bring clear direction and patterns of growth in both the natural and social realms. Your creative manifestation may revolutionize society in some way. Realize the great contrast between the inertial lag of human consciousness and the authentic services which enable human freedom. Offer services that make people realize that sharing transport and communication methods is necessary if humanity is not to be overcome by its own toxic waste.

Paths of Old Earth Spiritual Practises
(Essence Axis)

9 Soul Polarity:
(21 Love - 24 Shadows)

This path gives you the practise to see blind-spots and shadows in your soul. This will free your soul of conflict, for you will cease blaming others for any problems you have. Accept the tension between love and denial or fear as part of the process of the spiritual practise of equanimity.

10 Channelling:
(18 Inspiration - 30 Reason)

As you open your soul to real inspiration you can bring inspired voices and visions down into articulations that others can understand. This path affirms the practise of projecting your spirit through your soul and communicating through your mind. Taking responsibility for this whole process is an integral part of this practise. This is not channeling the voice of God, but of your higher Self.

147

11 Contemplation:
(17 Intention - 32 Thought)

This path affirms the practise of getting in touch with your deep intention from before you were born and bringing it into full vision. Pure vision is spontaneous and a clear action of the spirit, whereas imagination is a voluntary act of the mind. You can now use both spirit and mind to bring your original intention down into pure contemplative thought. You can then tap into universal intelligence.

12 Destiny Lineage:
(6 Cosmic Egg - 54 Awareness)

This path guides your practise of spiritual receptivity, evolutionary memory and karmic acceptance. As you open yourself to the full potential of universal life by means of intuition you can be aware of your ancestry back through your parents to the whole evolutionary lineage you've developed over various incarnations. Part of the practise of being aware of your destiny is accepting the exact ancestry, environment and circumstance in which you find yourself. You have the perfect context to fulfill your spiritual potential in this life.

13 Individuation:
(5 Source - 56 Integration)

You have infinite potential but are limited by your perception of life. As you feel the divinity in being human you can see the divine in others and undergo critical changes that can lead to individuation. This path guides you to the practise of activating vital intensity so that your body circulates subtle energy to the point of "miraculous" healing. Such healing can change your perception so that you can see the divine in everyone and feel the wholeness of your individuated self.

14 Voluntary Surrender:
(2 Divine Eye - 62 Creativity)

This path shows that you are more and more surrendering to a divine vantage and you can initiate processes involving the higher mind. Practise meditation with the intent to receive greater clarity on the cosmic plan inherent in the human being as a microcosm. You may experience conflict or even bodily pain, but this is the practise of creative self-transformation so that you can actualize the divine while being human. Practise surrendering your self-will to the plan your higher mind reveals while using will in powerful creative ways according to that higher plan.

15 Liberating Communion:
(1 Eternity to 64 Freedom)

As you find the balance and spiritual energy to make sacrifices, enabling you to commune with the eternal sources of all universes you will free yourself of self-limitation. Practise opening to the revelation that the source is in all things, that divinity is in every action. This path guides you to being open to cosmic law and to releasing relative conditions that hinder the greater purpose of the liberation of all beings from ignorance. Freedom is not following your likes and dislikes (which only lead to addictions), but in practising awareness of how things actually are.

16 Courageous Public Service:
(3 Spiritual Fire - 63 Service)

As you have the courage to enter intense spiritual practises which empower you to work in the world, you can develop the stable intent to go through all kinds of trials. You can use mass media or technologies in existing cultures to communicate about your services. This path affirms your power to use the tools and methods of the world in service of humanity as a whole. You may use some mathematical processes. Your own spiritual quest is a necessary part of your service. The polarity of spiritual quest and being in the world may bring trials, but you can now make clear justice work.

17 Revealing Perennial Wisdom:
(9 Guidance - 60 Regeneration)

This path guides you to have a deep awareness of the spiritual roots of all viable cultures in a perennial wisdom. You now have the capacity to initiate this awareness in discovering the seed-patterns of ancient and tribal cultures. You might work in fields of history, archeology, anthropology, or some form of shamanism. Geometry, divination, sacred mapping of worlds, ley lines - are part of this practise. Extract the perennial wisdom out of the ancient and tribal traditions and make a clear record of your findings. You may also be directly involved with living tribal peoples and bring the sacred practises and laws you discover into some form of neo-shamanism to help regenerate the modern social world.

18 Revolutionary Harmonics:
(11 Order - 59 Revolution)

You have the capacity to research and practise all kinds of harmonic orders of resonance and social order. Using sound, color, form, number or movements you can use these vibrational qualities in rituals to revolutionize some aspect of society. You may study resonance patterns, the arrangements of elements, color and forms in space as in mandalas and yantras. Study of ancient, medieval, and tribal architecture and the design of cities is a very relevant practise now. Examine the history of civilizations for the critical periods of change from one way of life to another and the underlying causes of these revolutions.

19 Pantheistic Shamanism:
(33 Vortex - 48 Consciousness)

You now have the capacity to enter the sources of nature with clear consciousness and to see the hierarchies of nature. This path affirms your practise of seeing spirit in nature and divinity in every planet, star, stone and flower. Knowing the immanence of divinity empowers you towards shamanic practises and ecological action. Planetary consciousness is a central part of your spiritual practise especially when you practise global awareness.

20 Biorhythms:
(35 Time - 47 Growth)

You can now be in rhythm with things through cycles. Practise being aware of your pulse, breath and walking rhythms. Feel out your mental, physical and emotional cycles as well as looking at astrological considerations. This path reveals the relation of birth to death, of growth to decay, and how all things increase and decrease in cycles. You can now develop a sense of timing with respect to hierarchies of larger and smaller cycles so as to recirculate vital energy throughout your being. You can be attuned to nature as a whole.

21 Vibrational Ground:
(41 Energy - 44 Direction)

As you work with and study the energy systems of nature you can understand and feel the vibrational ground of matter. Physics or astrophysics might give you a deeper understanding of the cosmic laws of matter and antimatter. The charge and direction of spin in fundamental "particles" can be examined. As you realize that matter is the most changing aspect of existence, you can experience your ground as a sea of vibrations which paradoxically supports your life.

Paths of Old Earth Experience
(Existence Axis)

22 Spiritual Radiance:
(3 Spiritual Fire - 2 Divine Eye)

You have direct experience with a large spiritual perspective. You can see clairvoyantly and you can transform your life through spiritual fire. You can now learn through high illumination within your own experience.

23 Illuminative Guidance:
(9 Guidance - 5 Source)

This path shows that you are being guided in transformation by the primal, spiritual sources of the universe. Be aware of your own spiritual energy and practise meditation. You may experience illumination as a sign that your own aura is clearing and expanding. You may take an interest in ancient traditions or myths and symbols as a mirror of what you are experiencing.

24 Initiating New Order:
(11 Order - 6 Cosmic Egg)

You have the power to move with the spiritual sources of the universe and see the great potential in everything you see or touch. You are having an experiential initiation through your own courage to move ahead with the spiritual practises you are involved in. Look into harmonic orders of color, sound, movement, form and number so that you can be an initiator of others in one or more of these fields.

25 Sacred Native Traditions:
(33 Vortex - 17 Intention)

You are coming into your spiritual intention and as you find clarity you will discover the infinite possibilities in your life for bringing balance into nature. You are having direct experience of how the subtle levels of life are the sources of nature and how the sacred traditions of tribal and ancient peoples were in touch with these same sources. You can commune with trees, stars and soils to ask the nature spirits what would nurture them. And when you need to change terrain or take life for food or shelter, ask the nature spirits—for they know your true intention.

26 Expressing the Divine Plan:
(35 Time - 18 Inspiration)

You have the capacity to directly experience inspiration about the divine plan. You can bring your inspiration into greater manifestations by using lights, sound and waves of all kinds to stimulate growth. Light shows, music, color or dance are all possible media to use to express what you see of the divine plan. The timing of when you do what is important. Be aware of certain seasons, times of the day or night. Look at critical changes in the life cycles of others. You can create events now.

27 Cosmic Love:
(41 Energy - 21 Love)

As you love more you can have direct visions into imaginal reality and can realize the connection between the imaginal domains and those of astrophysics. Mapping the outer world of the vastly large galactic and stellar systems and also the micro-realms of atomic energy is relevant now. You may find that these outer realms are also inner and that the human being is a microcosm of nature as the macrocosm. Love is the central transformer of your life now, for without it you could not have the energy to experience what you do. See that love, energy and stars are all one, and your offering to the world will be great.

28 Incarnate Transformation:
(43 Inertia - 22 Desire)

This path reveals that you are both grounded and protected because you can directly experience how desire creates its own object. This means that your protection resides in the fact that you realize that incarnation in a physical body is a temporary state. You may be dying in some way, for through release of any attachments to matter and the body you realize the limitation of existence. On the other hand you can attract any matter - even another body in another incarnation - through projection of your desires. Give thanks to you parents and ancestors and move on. Everything is in an extreme state of change and transformation so that you can learn the polarity of the birth and death of desire.

29 Sacred Earth Geometry:
(44 Direction - 24 Shadows)

Now is a good time to have a concern with the solar system and planet as a whole. You can find and practise forms of geometry and earth divination to help heal the earth, resulting from human spoilation. You can help rectify the confusion that has resulted from human blind spots and shadows by using your life energy and imagination in sacred geometry related to the earth. Power places, ley lines, city planning, designing gardens, parks and schools - are all ways for your learning and growth now.

30 Management of Resources:
(47 Growth - 30 Reason)

You can now have direct experience with gardening, self cultivation, animal husbandry or work with the elements in any form. This path empowers you to go through any conflicts resulting from involvements with doing things in the world of law, agriculture, economics, art of social science. Remember the lessons you learned in the past and use your rational mind to evaluate experiments and experiences, and to find new methods of procedure so that there is a better management of resources.

31 Generation Transmission:
(48 Consciousness - 32 Thought)

As you become more conscious of the direction and purpose of life you will have greater power to change ancestral habits by asking what is right in each situation and releasing outworn habits. Use your mind in its fullest capacity to find ways to heal past personal social errors and to create new traditions that transmit ethical values to future generations. This path guides you to the transmission of clear thought to children.

32 Media Revolution:
(59 Revolution - 54 Awareness)

You can now be aware of the influence of society on the individual and vice versa. You can learn about different cultures and see how the will and awareness of certain powerful individuals changed the current of history. But the inertia of traditions is great. Witness the uniformity resulting from mass production and see how technologies can be used by people rather than people used by technologies. You can now be aware of how individual expression is limited and conditioned by how others think, by habits, advertising, politics and mass media. This can lead you to seeing how to revolutionize society by its own methods in a direction of wholeness.

33 Mirroring Self and Society:
(60 Regeneration - 56 Integration)

This path reveals your power to begin to regenerate society through the integration of your spirit, psyche and body. As you directly experience many cultures, races, creeds, nations and ways of governing people you can see how different ways of life are like the different functions of your own life. These insights can bring you into an ecstasy which is the reward and clear sign of regenerating society and integrating your self.

34 Art:
(63 Service - 62 Creativity)

You now have the capacity to serve other forms of life according to their need. The art of seeing what is needed and finding ways to fulfill needs is turning adversity to advantage. Your creativity is paramount needed now, for this path reveals that you can apply art to any situation - whether painting, music or a creative business venture.

Paths of Old Earth Governance
(Vertical)

35 Radiant Hierarchy:
(1 Eternity - 43 Inertia)

This path guides you to heal at a distance radionically, while attuned to subtle vibrations. You might work with some aspect of the electromagnetic spectrum as a governor of how the subtle forces work into the grosser and denser levels of existence. Use music, architecture, astronomy and mathematics and see how these harmonic ordering forces shape culture. Observe how cycles of many sorts are governors of energy-flow into matter and back again into energy. Life cycles, seasonal cycles, the rhythms of the heartbeat and of the vibrations of strings or oscillators are all governors of the radiant hierarchy of nature. You can govern by being in harmony with cycles.

36 Natural Governance:
(2 Divine Eye - 44 Direction)

Your perspective and spiritual awareness is very great. Now you can see the heart of the sacred tradition that lies in the core of every atom and star. Have the courage to enact what you see, and bring your spiritual vision down through the resonant star fields into the matter of everyday life. You might study physics or astronomy, looking into the heart of matter and seeing how the direction of spin or orbiting makes a difference to the fate of an entity. You can govern by bringing spiritual vision into matter and directing your life in accordance with hierarchies of nature.

37 Invisible Ecology:
(5 Source - 47 Growth)

As you quest for the sources of things, you can find seed-patterns of the governance of life in invisible domains. Keep balanced and aligned with spiritual sources and you will be able to discover spheres of key designs that can be applied to architecture or the understanding of plant and animal morphology. Ecological concerns for the planet as a whole may include the study of soils, agriculture, weather patterns, migration and urban effects on nature. You can govern through this path by being aware of reciprocal life exchanges, the food chain, energy transfer and practising what you learn as an ecological planetary involvement.

37 Dimensional Economy:
(6 Cosmic Egg - 48 Consciousness)

This path can guide you to applying spiritual laws to economical methods of either producing or consuming products that can change people's consciousness. Be aware that all parts of the cosmos are interconnected and therefore what you send out into the world will come back to you in some way. Mathematics - especially geometry - may help in designing and displaying the forms of the products you are involved in producing or marketing. You may work in many different dimensions. Dimensional economy is governing by using the least amount of elements for optimal quality of a given product and finding products in harmony with the spiritual laws of infinite resourcefulness.

38 Spiritual Ethics:
(17 Intention - 59 Revolution)

This path can guide you to govern yourself and others by being in touch with your spiritual intention and intuition while working in the world. This may involve many trials and difficulties with generations, ancestors, and old ways of doing things - but if you hold to your truth, outworn ways of life will be revolutionized. You may use images to reveal the difference between ethical and unethical ways of life. Justice is the governor of this path and you may find models of how justice works in the human body by the necessity for limits and boundaries for each interconnected body system.

39 Technology and Magic:
(18 Inspiration - 60 Regeneration)

This path shows that you have clear inspiration and vision rising from powerful vital energy, and that you can govern your family, community, research or business by staying in touch with your own conscience. The challenge of this path is the possible conflict involved when the self comes into direct experience with both real inspiration and the repetitive, mundane world. You can use mass media, advertising or technical equipment to either receive or send information. You might be interested in genetics, engineering, social science or law. You can influence others by expressing your interest in what values regenerate society. Use advertising by appealing to people's true empowerment rather than what makes them addicted.

40 Arts and Healing:
(21 Love - 63 Service)

You can govern best now by loving more deeply, for love is not blind, but sees and has the power to heal ancient wounds. This path guides you to be aware of your own projections and therefore empowers you to direct imagination by clear will rather than reactiveness. The ecstasy that comes when you let love be the governor of the art of life is its own reward. You can use any of the arts as a service to humanity to open deep remembrance of human purpose and to exercise the imagination.

41 Creative Depth Psychology:
(22 Desire - 64 Freedom)

This path can guide you to face your own shadows and blind spots and use clarity of thought to become aware of things you may have denied. This will empower you to be a guide to others in doing the same. As you come into your own integration of mind, soul, and body you will open great avenues of creativity. You might either be counselled in matters of the psyche or counsel others. As you become a governor of your own life, there will be true freedom, which comes only by taking complete responsibility for your life.

NEW EARTH
Paths of New Earth Governance
(Vertical)

42 Balanced Education:
(65 Giving - 107 Responsibility)

This path can empower you to take responsibility for actually building new centers of clear awareness in communities or building new models of education that will give people insight on the priorities in their life. The balance of the male and female within you is an important part of this path since you will be tested in any masculine or feminine dominance or reactiveness you have. Acknowledge past mistakes and work with others in giving form to new educational processes.

43 Pyschological Healing:
(66 Devotion - 108 Resurrection)

The purity of your devotion to the vision you have of the New Earth can be measured in the capacity you have to forgive yourself and others for past mistakes and to come into a loving receptivity of the new. Release the past and discover the poetry in your heart which can empower you to create new cultural possibilities. The marriage of opposites within you will be an empowerment for deep psychological healing.

44 Technological Incorporation:
(73 Individuality - 111 Sublimation)

The more true to yourself you are, the more you reveal individuality and the more you can be wholehearted with others. This self-empowerment can extend to others through technologies which are self-regenerating and free of toxic waste products. You may either communicate through such technologies or design them and arrange for them to be built. Through these New Earth means you will alleviate a great deal of potential suffering for humanity as a whole and bring joy to many.

45 Global Community:
(70 Cooperation - 112 Consummation)

Through cooperation with peoples from diverse races, cultures, governments and creeds you will be able to find the keys towards a global self-actualized society. This path opens you to a vast network of peoples, all of whom are part of a great living body. As you are open to truth you will find methods of diplomacy and ways to communicate the sincerity of your own spiritual practise of integrity. Absolute integrity is demanded to bring together nations in a consummation. Fulfillment will come through a burning of interferences.

46 Spiritual Service:
(81 Illumination - 123 Oneness)
This path enables you to see that light is inherent in all life and stimulates you to come into your own illumination. This illuminated vision of life will activate a deep transformation in your body that can then effect the healing of nature. As you surrender to the process of intensifying energy you will be able to create rituals and services which reciprocate the gifts of light and life back to the oneness that gave them forth. Such spiritual services will have great reverberations in the lives of others.

47 Practical Wisdom:
(82 Rebirth - 124 Being)
This path brings you to a death and rebirth which enables you to bring forth new ways of using light and color in practical ways. Your own radiance will be a sign of your awakening to nature's flowing metamorphic life. As you see pure being in all sentient beings you will have the flexibility to awaken and appreciate the inherent nature of each unique being. The practicality of your innate wisdom will be revealed by how much you first accept everything just as it is. Only then can it be transformed.

48 Sacred Art:
(85 Remembering - 127 Everywhere)
As you gather your essence together you will remember who you really are and can see the dawn of the New Earth everywhere. Concentrate all your abilities, attention and energy towards actualizing the vision you have of the New Earth. Then listen for the music inherent in all things. The new art and music will be born out of your great trust in the harmony of the universe on all levels whereby the sacred tradition will be reactivated through sacred art.

49 Practising Peace:
(86 Fearless - 128 Compassion)
This path reveals the essence of your light-body to be the source of turning all past karma into a fearless constancy of spirit. As you practise equanimity you will experience the harmony in nature, and a harmonic basis for developing relationships by deep resonance. You may hear music as part of this process. The cosmic sound current manifests through harmonies which can heighten humanity's experience of compassion. As you turn any poison in the world to medicine you will have the luminosity to practise peace in all your relations.

Paths of Experiencing the New Earth
(Existence Axis)

50 Joyous Building:
(66 Devotion - 67 Construction)
This path shows that you can volunteer to build new models of culture through the devotion in your heart. Keep the central flame of devotion ardent and your work will have joy even in the midst of adversity. You are taking steps towards the actual construction of models for a Celestial Earth. The reward of your work is intrinsic joy.

51 Sexual Balance:
(69 Individuality - 73 Androgyne)
The power of your individuality is strengthened by the androgynous fusion of the masculine and feminine within your soul. Make impeccable your motives as you work with others in envisioning and actualizing the New Earth in your relationships. The purity of your intentions will strengthen the equitable balance of both men and women—as well as the masculine and feminine qualities in your relationships.

52 Human Empowerment:
(70 Cooperation - 75 Clarity)
You have great clarity about human relationships which transcends

material, cultural, and racial boundaries. You can empower others now because you are grounded in your own authentic power. Use new technologies to spread crosscultural relations in a spirit of cooperation. Emphasis on the complementary qualities of different peoples might be expressed through dramatic enactments or art expression.

53 Social Self-Actualization:
(81 Illumination - 97 Insight)

You can now realize that as nature becomes more and more regenerated through consciousness, there will be insight on the purpose of life. This insight comes through the union of heart and mind when there is confession of any past illusion or falsehood. Realize that the soul of culture is whole and luminous. A self-actualized society will take place through the marriage of opposites in the soul of peoples of diverse cultures. Your insight about the illuminated consciousness of the masses will be very beneficial.

54 New Perspectives:
(82 Rebirth - 99 Brilliance)

You are now guided to pass through narrow openings. If you walk with complete integrity you will have a rebirth into the light of the supernal sun and can see from new perspectives. Then you might discover how light is the circulation system of the natural universe and create methods of solar ecology. The brilliance of your own mind is linked with your heart and the heart of the sun. As you realize this, your life will itself become poetry in action.

55 Alignment with Truth:
(85 Remembering - 105 Acknowledge)

As you remember yourself before you were born you will experience a radical transformation of your energy. The heightened energy will lead to a great receptivity to greater truth. As your light-body develops you will be able to raise the vibrational level of the plants and animals around you with pure radiance. Give whole-hearted acknowledgement to anything you've denied in the past and your soul, body and mind will align with truth, naturally and effortlessly.

56 Responsive Embodiment:
(86 Fearless - 107 Responsibility)

Gathering together the qualities of your true self you can now walk fearlessly through any aspect of trepidation. As you meet obstacles, surrender to the higher vibration energy and cease any resistance. You can experience the vastness of all of sentience with the flowing energy of your own body. Then you will see how to rectify ecological imbalances. Realize that nature and your body are one. As you forgive any past wounding you will be empowered with a greater ability to respond to the true needs of nature and other people. Eventually you can incorporate this transformation in ecology in a New Earth institute or school.

57 Kundalini Clinics:
(88 Essence - 108 Resurrection)

The essence of your life is a very concentrated substance, ready to be ignited by your full awakening. This path guides you to discover that the root of suffering is in resistance to realizing that love is the power that can resurrect all souls. All bodies are within a universal cosmic body. You are awakening to this realization through the heightening of your own energy level whereby you can penetrate to the causes of things and help heal both humanity and nature. Gather together resources for a kundalini school or clinic where this realization can serve others.

58 Conscious Ritual:
(94 Constancy - 111 Sublimation)

This path guides you to practise deep self-acceptance and constancy in your life. As you listen to other people and the music inherent in nature, listen for the subtle levels of reality that go beyond the outward appearance and sensations of things. You can now see the sublime in nature and can find the repeated rhythms within your body, your routines, and the seasons. Give back to nature through a conscious ritualizing of these rhythms.

59 Trusting Nature and Spirit:
(96 Sound Current - 112 Consummation)

You stand at the very apex of the nature of the New Earth which is rooted in the wisdom of knowing that all effects reverberate in all kingdoms and levels of reality. When you hear the cosmic sound current as a high frequency sound that transcends all external sounds you are being guided to consummate your life. Trust the inherent harmony of the spiritual order and you can experience the ultimate effect of nature within your own spirit as a fulfillment of your intention.

60 Actualizing the Sacred Tradition:
(118 Harmony - 123 Oneness)

This path reveals your actualization of the New Earth through making tangible the harmonies inherent in the sacred tradition. You can realize the immense potential of the experience of the oneness of all things and thus become extremely flexible in how you interact with others and fulfill your work in creative harmonics. You can create music or forms of art in any modality to help actualize the New Earth spiritual culture. The sacred tradition is the perennial wisdom inherent in the core of all things. It is this core of harmony that enables you to experience oneness.

61 Spiritual Peace Presence:
(120 Peace - 124 Being)

You are now guided to a transcendent experience of pure being whereby you can experience great peace. Extend this peace to others through your spiritual aura. You can truly emanate the subtle spiritual qualities of peace and help bring to consciousness the subtle energy forms that support all things. You can see the dawn of the New Earth and contribute to it through the dynamism of your spiritual presence.

62 Illumination:
(126 Luminosity - 127 Everywhere)

This path reveals that you are living in an immanent luminosity that enables you to have true spiritual vision. This experience will become central to your whole life and will enable you to access spiritual illumination far beyond dimensional considerations. Yet it will spread its influence through all dimensions. As you live more and more in illumination you will be one with illuminated beings everywhere.

Paths of New Earth Spiritual Practises
(Essence Axis)

63 Releasing and Remembering:
(85 Remembering - 88 Essence)

The essence of your whole life is emerging by your dying to all habits and ways of life that interfere with the quickening of your light-body. You can remember past incarnations as a process of releasing any attachment to particular stances, identities, or images. So let it all go and allow cellular changes to a higher frequency level of life, even if it means a passing beyond matter.

64 Healing Nourishment:
(82 Rebirth - 94 Constancy)

The rebirth of light within you entails a breakdown and regathering of essential qualities that can heal both you and the sentience around you. Develop constancy in your daily routines and spiritual practises. Extend the constancy of care to nurture plants and animals as well as people around you. Be aware of your regular diet, exercise, fresh air and light vibrations. All forms of nourishment—from the lowest to the highest—are needed now.

65 Light and Sound Healing:
(81 Illumination - 96 Sound Current)

This path shows that you have developed a radiance that is one with the New Earth and that this radiance can be a source of illumination within others. You can concentrate your life into a single focus and thereby make breakthroughs in your healing and wholeness. In addition, you can use this concentration to develop solar ecology and methods of using high frequency sound for healing.

66 Harmonic Perspectives:
(70 Cooperation - 118 Harmony)

As you work with others in cooperation you can have a new perspective on how light and sound can be used as healing agents and for power in cities of great wholeness. Listen to the harmonics of the universe in whatever way harmony comes to you—music, the structure of plants, chemistry, visual patterns or formal property. Then you can design new forms of social interaction using the translation of harmonics as a basis.

67 Synarchic Dynamics:
(69 Individuality - 120 Peace)

This path shows that you are so grounded in your individuality that you can awaken to intense levels of energy. This intense subtle energy can transform both you and the society around you. Share with others in your community the changes you are experiencing and work on bringing about a world peace. Trust that each individual's awakening helps others awaken also. New forms of social interaction and methods of using social tensions creatively and dynamically will naturally come to you. Then the New Earth Synarchical government can begin to actualize world peace.

68 Self-Accepting Ethics:
(66 Devotion - 126 Luminosity)

As you devote yourself to finding new methods of technology to spread the luminosity of spiritual happiness to others you will actualize deep self-acceptance. Create an ethical basis for the new technology and surrender to the Love-Light. You can actualize new communication, transport and entertainment by wise use of ethical values, money, and means of transactions between divergent peoples. Consider the value of what programs are to be exchanged between nations. What plays, music and art would you sponsor?

69 Reciprocal Abundance:
(65 Giving - 128 Compassion)

As you purify your life by clear confessions, asking for truth only, you will magnify your abundance on all levels. This path guides you to make appropriate offerings to all kinds of people you meet and to arrange for beneficial imports and exports between people or nations.

You wisdom of management can be measured by the truth of your own compassion for humanity as a whole. Make no show of your spiritual motives, but keep them constantly in the forefront of your intention in global transactions and you will see the dawn of the New Earth.

70 Constructive Distribution:
(67 Construction - 127 Everywhere)

This is a path of powerful building of the New Earth as a passage to true reciprocity between divergent realms and different cultures. Practise flexibility while maintaining a plan with the aim of overall transmission of information and commodities throughout the world. Examine new methods of construction, whereby the central networking system spreads everywhere, including subtle and material levels of existence. The power of distribution comes from flexible plans and vast vision.

71 Erotic Spirituality:
(73 Androgyne - 124 Being)

As you realize how deep the fusion of all opposites is within you, there will be reverberations of the spiritual within the cultural and sexual levels of the New Earth. You can help in the marriage of many opposing points of view. You can then be a counsellor of couples who are seeking to find new social forms for sexual fulfillment. Be wholehearted in your being and a whole body of peoples will come forth to manifest the marriage of the masculine and feminine polarities within individuals, couples and societies.

72 Diversity in Unity Incorporated:
(75 Clarity - 123 Oneness)

This path reveals that you have gained great clarity about your own wholeness. Therefore you can write and speak in poetry that can bond groups in common spiritual practises. You may create a business or institute to structure and contain the practises you discover. Literary expressions of the great potential of the ideal of diversity in unity will help consolidate your purpose now.

73 Living Your Bliss:
(97 Insight - 112 Consummation)

As you are receptive you will gain insight on the meaning of your life. Any suffering you have experienced is a beneficial sign, a natural feedback from the program of life so that you can gain insight on the limits of selfish concerns. As you embrace any pain you may have you can transmute suffering into a life consummation. Burn through all dross and interference to receptive realization of the meaning of your life. This is *living* you bliss.

74 Sublime Discrimination:
(99 Brilliance - 111 Sublimation)

The brilliance of your mind can only be fully known through heart-mind unity. Forgive yourself and others any errors of the past. Sift the wheat from the chaff in all your methods of relating to others. Discrimination is not a judgemental blame, but a release of all blame and a refining process of bringing your brilliance into a sublime act of clearing and prioritizing. You can know your true values only from a sublime perspective.

75 Loving Acknowledgement:
(105 Acknowledge - 108 Resurrection)

Being on this path assures you that, as you acknowledge shadows and blind spots, your soul will be completely cleansed. You will then feel great love for all beings. This is nothing less than burning through old doubt and denial, and a full soul resurrection through the power of love.

Paths of the New Earth Creative Process
(Horizontal)

76 Social Ecology:
(65 Giving - 86 Fearless)

When you realize your oneness with the earth and other human beings, the illumination within you will bring a rebirth of benevolence. With this path you can open doors to the New Earth fearlessly. Remember your vow before you were born and work with devotion towards a cooperative society. Your individuality will be revealed the more you give to the common good.

77 Building and Communicating:
(67 Construction - 88 Essence)

You can now build new organizations or new forms of architecture, or designs that come out of common needs with others. Mass media of various kinds - television, magazines, computer games, radio - can be used to transmit the utility and value of the models you are building. New technologies—especially in the use of sunlight for energy—can be explored. This path opens you to seeing the essence of everything and enables you to gather the corporate structures and resources needed to execute new designs in society.

78 Constancy Amidst Change:
(73 Androgyne - 94 Constancy)

Now you have self-empowerment through the balance and deep fusion of the male and female within you. Make clear confession to any imbalances of male or female dominance or reactivity. Then the quickening energy you feel will flow through you and open your chakras effortlessly. Expect changes both within and without and practise constancy from the deepest levels of your being. You can then concentrate and focus your life towards a healing of society and nature.

79 Sound Ethics:
(75 Clarity - 96 Sound Current)
This path shows that you have largely been true to yourself and have moved through conflict. Therefore you have the clarity to be a harbinger of values—the ethical patterns and laws that can help others to come to their truth. Then you can awaken to such a degree that your very presence will heal nature through vast fields of energy that are resonant with the root of nature herself. Listen to the songs of plants, animals and minerals and you will hear the music inherent in matter as well as the harmonic sources of nature which are beyond the senses.

80 Trusting Your Poetry:
(97 Insight - 118 Harmony)
As you have greater insight into the meaning of life as a whole you will be able to bring the poetry of your heart into the lives of others. Being wholehearted you will be able to experience your body as a vast presence or subtle energy that includes all sentience. Make offerings of resources, time and skills to groups or individuals who are worthy - for this is an act of true self-acceptance. Trust the harmony of the universe that you know in your heart and the balance of giving and receiving will be found.

81 Global Networking:
(99 Brilliance - 120 Peace)
You can incorporate many different cultures, life-styles, races and creeds into one whole. As you become more receptive to others you can express your wisdom in brilliant methods for the purpose of actualizing peace. You can then help bring about new urban plans in the New Earth. Divergent tendencies can be organized within a global network which takes into account differences like different organs within a whole body.

82 Transmutation:
(105 Acknowledge - 126 Luminosity)
Any suffering you may have now is simply part of the pathos of being human. Such suffering can be transmuted by acknowledging your own shadows and blind-spots and forgiving yourself and others all past wounding. As such transmutation becomes a constant practise your life

will have reverberations on spiritual levels of reality which will show in the luminosity of your aura. By a constant practise of transmutation you will become very flexible in changing life situations and be able to release any rigid habits and help spiritualize the whole earth.

83 Spiritual Fulfillment:
(107 Responsibility - 128 Compassion)

This path opens you to your fullest spiritual fulfillment through your ability to respond to other's real needs. You can take more responsibility the more you bring your desires back into love. As you separate the gross and refined elements in your life your love will bring sublimity to others and you will be able to consummate your life in a state of great compassion. This compassionate response comes out of the oneness of pure being which shines everywhere, on all alike.

Medicine Planes

There are not only Medicine Paths within the Old Earth and within the New Earth, but there are Medicine Planes *between* them. Over a period of time, or even in one sitting of inquiry, you may pick the same Vibrational Healing Card, but in the opposite orientation (Old Earth becomes New Earth or vice versa). This is a Plane. Any mixture of Old Earth and New Earth cards that aligns horizontally, vertically, or diagonal is also a plane. That is, if you pick a mixture of Old and New Earth cards, transpose either the New to Old *or* the Old to New and they then fall on a path, that makes the *original mixture* a plane.

Imagine the Medicine Planes as interdimensional doorways between the worlds which you walk when you become either more global and holistic (New Earth) or more working with the Old Earth world order—sometimes out of necessity and sometimes out of compassion.

Planes Between Old Earth and New Earth
(Existence)

84 Radiant Luminosity:
(2 Divine Eye to 127 Luminosity or 3 Spiritual Fire to 126 Everywhere)

You are one with the first act of creation. When spiritual fire streams through you, luminosity spreads and you can see through the divine eye, which is everywhere. Be in the light and be light and you will see.

85 Guiding Presence:
(9 Guidance to 124 Being or 5 Source to 120 Peace)

As you access the primal spiritual source, you can get in touch with pure being. Follow your deepest guidance and the aura of God will permeate your aura. This will bring forth a dawn of the true peace within your being. Be. Be guided and experience peace.

86 Acts of Sacred Order:
(6 Cosmic Egg to 118 Harmony or 11 Order to 123 Oneness)

You now have the courage to actualize your full potential harmoniously and vibrationally. Let the vibration and potency within you implode towards a center of order. Remain flexible as you begin to sing, dance, use color and hear the symphony of life. These vibrational harmonics are ever present and accessible everywhere, anytime. Actualize the inherent harmony of the universe.

87 Sacred Trust:

(33 Vortex to 112 Consummation or 17 Intention to 96 Sound Current)

Remembering your true intention, your life vow, and staying in balance opens you to receive the perennial wisdom. Perennial wisdom is the source of all enduring world culture. As you trust yourself and the roots of culture you may access the source of nature and hear the cosmic sound current. This means that infinity will reverberate within you as wisdom opens you to the sacred traditions. This is where the river of true culture runs clear and cosmic harmonies can be heard. In this state your life vow can be consummated.

88 Practising Reciprocity:

(18 Inspiration to 94 Constancy or 35 Time to 111 Sublimation)

Listening to your inspiration and intuition can become a constant spiritual practise. As your quest shifts into true self acceptance, the divine plan for human fulfillment will be open to you. Reciprocity is returning to God the gift of life through creativity and new life. Listening to the resonant cycles of nature can elevate you to sublime states of inspiration. As you consciously practise listening, self acceptance and reciprocity you will transcend time through constancy.

89 Love Resurrected:

(21 Love to 88 Essence or 41 Energy to 108 Resurrection)

Through love your vision expands with clarity. Love is not blind, love sees the fulfillment of the God-given human image through the cosmic body. By empathy through your cosmic body you can feel the oneness with all sentient life. Use the light and patterns of the stars as a matrix of seed ideas to actualize the human image as cosmic love. What in ancient times was sacrifice (to make sacred), is now an offering to assist in the awakening of humanity. As you transform energy into essence your offering will transmute suffering and the human soul will be resurrected.

90 Responsible Incarnation:

(22 Desire to 86 Fearlessness or 43 Inertia to 107 Responsibility)

The whole of your life stream embodiment is being transformed. Addictive tendencies are transforming into fearless, responsive redemption. To continue in this process is to realize how your desires have created the succession of incarnations leading to your present constitution and circumstances. Forgive past blame and hurt. Give thanks to your ancestors and fully incorporate all peoples and sentient life into the field of your cosmic body. Surrender to the kundalini energy flowing through your body. Fearlessly move through the past of accumulated resistance and inertia. Experience the flow of space and higher realities. Then new dimensions will open unto you.

91 Planetary Truth:

(24 Shadows to 85 Remembering or 44 Direction to 105 Acknowledge)

As you find direction through the remembrance of your true purpose, you can penetrate the shadows of your soul and release imaginary fears. Feel your fears and go to the bottom of them. Acknowledge what you have previously denied and be receptive to what is. Fear and illusion will be dispelled. As you change intensity into wholeheartedness, you can live the truth more fully and help transform the planet through the radiance of your being. Behold the laws of form as a sacred geometry that is alive and flowing rather than rigid. You can help heal the planet through the transformation of your own mind, body and soul.

92 Resourceful Perspectives:

(47 Growth to 99 Brilliance or 30 Reason to 82 Rebirth)

Through long trials and self conflict you are opening the passageways between your mind and the natural environment. As you work with the animals, plants and elements, allow yourself to see the light in all life. Perceive how you can facilitate the light into a solar ecology. Cease trying to figure things out, heighten your perceptions and share in the universal brilliance. See how trials of the past become doorways linking humanity and nature through ethics. Past memories are being vivified as poetry as you behold the meaning of life, and as you create pathways to bring light technologies into human culture.

93 Conscious Ethics:
(32 Thought to 81 Illumination or 48 Consciousness to 97 Insight)

As you become conscious of the impact of past generations you may become aware of considerations for future generations. Now is a time to profoundly confess your own and others' errors of past generations. This will bring insight into the healing process. Be aware of the balance of the masculine and feminine within every soul, society and nature. Be conscious of the integrity of all actions and you will be illumined while the inner marriage takes place. This inner marriage contributes to bringing forth social harmony as synarchy. The social and spiritual work you do now, concerning the marriage of opposites—within the self and within society—will greatly benefit future generations.

94 Social Change:
(59 Revolution to 75 Clarity or 70 Cooperation to 54 Awareness)

In competitive societies, will is used to overpower others. You may be involved with the competitive use of will or with a system in which control revolves between various powers via the vehicle of force. Now is the time to change self-will into the true empowerment of love-will. Love-will transforms endless revolutions into cooperation. Your awareness may now be clarified. Use technology as a means rather than an end. Create a system in which the offerings of all are received as valuable contributions to the benefit of the whole.

95 Individuation:
(56 Integration to 69 Individuality or 60 Regeneration to 73 Androgyne)

As you deepen the integration of the polarities within yourself, you will realize the androgyne of your inner nature. The balance of the masculine and feminine within your soul and in relationships can reveal ecstasy and purity. Regeneration and new social forms emerge through the strong, confident expressions of the individuals who maintain this inner balance.

96 Right Livelihood:
(66 Devotion to 62 Creativity or 67 Construction to 63 Service)

As you blend playful creativity with service to humanity you are approaching right livelihood in the Old Earth. When creativity becomes a step by step consistence construction of the New Earth, you will realize that service has become pure devotion. Devotion is ardent love and faith in practise. Be Devoted and Build according to your visions.

97 Voluntary Giving:
(64 Freedom to 65 Giving)
The path to freedom has been long and you are worthy. What will you do with this freedom? This is not freedom from anything, but freedom within the actualities that surround you. It is freedom in being one with the whole of life. As you realize this deep oneness you can initiate aspects of New Earth culture through the giving forth of your gifts. Giving opens the door through which you pass with freedom into the New Earth. Give what you no longer need to others. Give of your love, your awareness, and your labor. Giving in this spirit awakens the Love-Light.

Planes Between Old Earth and New Earth
(Horizontal)

98 Initiating Compassion:
(1 Eternity to 107 Responsibility or 22 Desire to 128 Compassion)
Initiating a creative process in the Old Earth can bring you closer to spiritual fulfillment in the New Earth. You can now change a narrow sense of desire into the open ability to respond. This depends on your clear intention to stay with sources, the oneness of pure being. Center yourself each moment and feel your connection to all sentient beings everywhere. Eternity will shine through your compassion.

99 Soul Clearing:
(3 Spiritual Fire to 105 Acknowledge or 126 Luminosity to 24 Shadows)
True vision is received through spiritual practises that burn through karma and suffering. Respond with flexibility to the intuitive spiritual impulses that come to you. Acknowledge anything you have feared or denied in the past. Forgive yourself and release holding blame that has been cast onto you or that you have projected onto others or yourself. You can now come into the light of a new dawn.

100 Peace Planning:
(9 Guidance to 99 Brilliance or 120 Peace to 30 Reason)

Use models, plans and designs to incorporate the wisdom you have gained throughout the ages. With courage you may now actualize that part of the divine plan that is seeded within you. Your reasoning may be permeated with flashes of brilliance. Realize that this brilliance is a divine gift and you can reciprocate with creative interest that with which you have been blessed. As you share your insight of the divine plan with others, you will bring peace unto the New Earth.

101 Poetic Relay:
(11 Order to 97 Insight or 118 Harmony to 32 Thought)

Trust in the streams of culture that come from the perennial wisdom. Offer the best of yourself in each situation that arises and old struggles will give way to self acceptance. Give of yourself in a wholehearted manner. Allow the intense memories of unfulfilled intention to emerge as insights, meaning and poetry. Let your poetry go forth into the world, for it is the expression of the new perennial culture.

102 Audible Truth:
(33 Vortex to 75 Clarity or 96 Sound Current to 54 Awareness)

The resonance of the universe is packaged in holograms. You have been perceptive of this and now it is time to surrender any identification with specific forms or ideas. Listen to the vibrations, the qualities as the sound of truth within all form. Realize that self conflict arises from attachment to specific ideas and objects. Reevaluate your life from the vantage of living your truth. Then your awareness will transform into a simple clarity of what is.

103 Regulating Power:
(35 Time to 73 Androgyne or 94 Constancy to 56 Integration)

As you integrate the polarities within yourself with consistency, self-will can transform into power through love-will. Concentrate and you will become radiant. As you work through your trials, you will find clear passage to living your truth. Step by step processes in time and space are the ways to transcend limitation. Ask for guidance and direction from the Divine and your life will become a flowing empowerment.

104 Constructive Gathering:
(41 Energy to 67 Construction or 88 Essence to 62 Creativity)
You can change the drab uniformity of the modern world into a radiant planet through the implementation of solar ecology. Appropriate technology can serve as a means to bring nations together in constructive gatherings. You might be involved in work with light and color. Purify yourself and the rarefied essence of your light body will contribute to the upliftment of social consciousness. The ancestral clans are changing into a crosscultural, interracial synarchy.

105 Changing Inertia:
(43 Inertia to 65 Giving or 86 Fearless to 64 Freedom
As you bring the Old Earth paradigms into manifestation, they become the ground for cooperation and giving. Overcome your resistance about severity and defense by facing what you fear. As you remember who you really are, your individuality will give you the confidence needed to cooperate with others. You have nothing to fear when you live your truth. Illuminate your consciousness and realize that the freedom to give is the giving of true freedom.

Planes Between Old Earth and New Earth
(Essence)
106 Soul Resurrection:
(21 Love to 105 Acknowledge or 108 Resurrection to 24 Shadows)
You know that the essence of your soul is love, but you are still blinded by your shadows. This prevents you from living from the essence of your soul. Acknowledge what you have denied in the past and resurrect your soul into its source as love. This can be done by trusting love and opening your heart. Let any pain be felt and it will vanish.

107 Spiritual Forgiveness:
(18 Inspiration to 99 Brilliance or 111 Sublimation to 30 Reason)
You can articulate your highest inspirations only when your soul is clear of blame and projection. As you forgive yourself and others for past wounding, the brilliance of your heart-mind unity will shine in your soul,

illuminating the sublimity of the spirit. Your life becomes refined as you are able to discern truth from falsehood and yet forgive.

108 Intentional Receptivity:
(17 Intention to 97 Insight or 112 Consummation to 32 Thought

Your spirit and mind can now become one. This is seeing clearly as in contemplating the reflection of the sky and mountains in a still lake. Enter the depths of life through your receptivity and embrace the suffering of humanity. It will then be consumed by the fires of insight and penetrating vision. This is like seeing the sun from the bottom of a clear lake shining through the waters of life.

109 Spiritual Family:
(6 Cosmic Egg to 75 Clarity or 123 Oneness to 54 Awareness)

You have remembered your true potential passed on to you through your ancestors. Lift these memories into meaning and they will become poetry. This will awaken you to the unity of all beings. Clarity activates empathic understanding. Practise taking action on your clear intuitions. Incorporate many types of people, cultures and ideas in your practises and celebrate the unity through diversity in life. All of humanity is ultimately your spiritual family.

110 Actualizing Being:
(5 Source to 73 Androgyne or 124 Being to 56 Integration)

Fulfillment in the God given human image is living wholeheartedly in each moment. You can access infinity through the divine dance of the masculine and feminine within. Be. Stay in the center of your being throughout the arousal of all fears and negative reactions. Thence your being will reach out to heal others and actualize the full potential of the human. Reverberations of this ecstatic wholehearted way of being will emanate to many others.

111 Creative Power:
(2 Divine Eye to 67 Construction or 62 Creativity to 127 Everywhere)

As you empower yourself, you will come into alignment with the divine plan. You will multiply and return the gifts you have been blessed with. Self conflict is to be seen as the opportunity to awaken you to the potential of your constructive creativity. Move through conflict by being strong, yet flexible, in your truth. You will gain divine perspective and your body will have a sense of fluidity and well-being.

112 Eternal Truth:
(1 Eternity to 65 Giving or 64 Freedom to 128 Compassion)
Pure essence is pervading your being. You realize that you will not arrive at your goal of freedom by avoiding problems and issues. Only through embracing and facing these challenges can compassion liberate you. As you *live* the truth, rather than merely know it, cosmic laws will be understood as the template through which freedom can be experienced. Otherwise law is seen as rules of restriction. Remain in balance and your wisdom will shine forth. Ask what will serve the whole in any situation and eternity will speak through your conscience. Ecstasy is found in purity and purity in ecstasy when you live the truth.

113 Multidimensional Technologies:
(3 Spiritual Fire to 66 Devotion or 126 Luminosity to 63 Service)
Your quest has revealed your courage in combining spirituality with mundane life, for this has involved many trials. This understanding can now be applied to New Earth technologies which can open doors to actualizing spiritual luminosity for many people. Maintain your devotion to people in ordinary daily life and surrender to the spiritual forces working through you. The deepest fulfillment is found in empowering others through your own presence.

114 New Cultural Forms:
(9 Guidance to 69 Individuality or 120 Peace to 60 Regeneration)
Tribes and clans are gathering and regrouping. It is imperative that you follow your guidance towards non-exclusive cultural change. Old forms are transforming. As you awaken with greater confidence into your true individuality, you will come into alignment with the perennial wisdom present throughout the ages of history. A higher order of new culture is now possible. You may help bring forth new forms of government and social organization. Trust in the inherent harmony of the universe and humanity will be one step closer to world peace. Peace can only be sustained by a peaceful people.

115 Paradigm Shifts:
(11 Order to 70 Cooperation or 118 Harmony to 59 Revolution)

Social change can be revolutionary or cooperative. Revolutionary change is often a competetive, manipulative act of force. Cooperation can be an all inclusive dynamic interplay of diverse qualities, nations, and races. Tune into the full spectrum of order and harmony in society and nature. From this greater perspective, experience how apparent dissonance shifts into consonance. Conflict and conflict resolution are a part of the drama involved in social, natural and spiritual change. Watch and listen with open eyes and ears and you will find yourself flowing with new orders of harmony beyond imagined possibilities.

116 Expanded Consciousness:
(33 Vortex to 81 Illumination or 96 Sound Current to 48 Consciousness)

You have plunged deeply into the sources of nature to commune with the spirits of the planet, stars and all of life. Now you can go beyond pantheism into a greater illumination within your consciousness. Light and sound are vibratory languages. The spirits of nature speak in these languages. Through the single pointed concentration of these vibratory languages, you can help heal the planet. In its wholeness you shall behold it's radiance and hear the cosmic sound current.

117 Constant Revivification:
(35 Time to 82 Rebirth or 94 Constancy to 47 Growth

In accepting incarnation you have entered into the density of earthly life, becoming one with time's cycles of growth and decay. Through change you can find constancy. Be reliable to yourself and master time. This will transform time into constancy. Gather together people and essences of your life that will precipitate a rebirth of being. Draw out the elixirs of divine breath in each stone, plant and beast and focus the energy towards the renewal of life on earth.

118 Light-Body Energetics:
(41 Energy to 85 Remembering or 88 Essence to 44 Direction

Energy is a gift from nature which you have harnessed in your body for the works and activities you pursue. The ways in which you have directed this energy have created the foundation from which you may now access your spiritual essence. Remember who you are, and that your soul is essentially immortal. As your body quickens on a cellular level, you will be able to remember the eternal essence of your being and release that which is old and outworn. You DNA may also be changing toward a heightened vibration.

119 Fearless Change:
(43 Inertia to 86 Fearless)
All that you have denied has made you inert and unable to change direction. As you face your fears, shadows and any being you have denied, you will become fearless. With fearlessness you will be able to move on and truly live your destiny.

Planes Between Old Earth and New Earth
(Vertical)

120 Resonant Transformation:
(1 Eternity to 86 Fearless or 43 Inertia to 128 Compassion)
The eternal source of guidance is opened unto you when the spiritual fires within yourself are kindled. Become attuned to the harmonies of the universe expressed through color, sound and form and you will experience the music of the spheres. Make constancy your friend and plunge into the depths of inertia through the transmutation of energy into essence. Face all resistance with fearlessness and you will become illumined. The power of compassion heals all sentient beings. Be in peace.

121 Resonating Trust:
(2 Divine Eye to 85 Remembering or 127 Everywhere to 44 Direction)
You have courageously brought forth the perennial wisdom in the past. Now you can trust that the roots of sacred tradition will bring forth new shoots. You can actualize the foundations of New Earth culture through concentration, listening and trust. Remember your true purpose and breathe in the Love-Light. Gather people and essences together to facilitate the grounding of higher frequencies onto the earth plane. Charge the Old Earth density with the brightness of the Love-Light. This will issue forth as perennial wisdom.

122 Planetary Flexibility:
(5 Source to 82 Rebirth or 124 Being to 47 Growth)
When you die to the outworn, you experience rebirth which brings greater radiance to the planet. Search and quest until you find true self acceptance. Remain in balance, then wisdom will lift you on the wings of pure being. This will enable you to apply your gifts to practical and planetary work. Flow with the process, and the seed ideas of long ago will awaken you to practical spirituality. Flowing increases your flexibility as you die and are reborn again and again. Then you will find that space is a context for movement.

123 Reciprocal Consciousness:
(6 Cosmic Egg to 81 Illumination or 123 Oneness to 48 Consciousness)
Consciousness is changed when you give form to the divine plan. With awakened consciousness you can tap into the infinite potential of spiritual sources. When consciousness becomes illumined you will know how to surrender to the transformations occurring within you. The divine source gives forth life and maintains all life. Realize the spiritual laws of reciprocity and make offerings. If you give with compassion, these offerings will reverberate throughout the spiritual and natural realms. Through reciprocity you will find oneness.

124 Intentional Cooperation:
(17 Intention to 70 Cooperation or 59 Revolution to 112 Consummation)
Ultimately, your intention, purpose and life vow is to fulfill the potential of the human image and consummate your life. You have undergone many trials in the past with ancestors, legal conflicts, social revolutions and cultural cataclysms. You have seen the limits of the Old Earth culture. As you begin to live in truth, trials will paradoxically open doorways to cooperation and synarchy (social harmony). Empathy with all sentient life will expand your experience of the bodily systems into the vastness of the cosmic body. This will fulfill the human images as the image of the divine. Exercise intuition as a spiritual practise and you will expand your conscious awareness of the truth. Your intention, purpose and life vow will then be consummated.

125 Ethical Embodiment:

(18 Inspiration to 69 Individuality or 111 Sublimation to 60 Regeneration)

The vital energy and intensity of your life is carried through inspiration and the genetic code. If you change intensity into wholeheartedness, you will be empowered. Use this power to inspire the poeple of a uniform society to access and utilize innovative forms of new technology. When applied appropriately, technology is a process that can hasten the passage of self-conflict into the right use of will. True confession can bring you into alignment with the divine. From the divine perspective technological incorporation can be implemented. Then suffering can be transformed to the sublimity.

126 Inner Marriage:

(21 Love to 66 Devotion or 108 Resurrection to 63 Service)

Will has been used to overcome the hurt and anger of lost love. True healing is in the realization of the wholeness within oneself. Dedicate yourself to the marriage of the male and female within yourself. Cease imaginary projections of fulfillment outside of your own being. Devote yourself to the process of purification and you will become receptive to the poetry of the soul. In the process you can forgive yourself for past errors. This can render willfulness into true power. Ancient wounds of the soul can be healed through true self empowerment. Resurrect the soul through love and you can be a governor of the new socio-spiritual order.

127 Responsive Freedom:

(22 Desire to 65 Giving or 107 Responsibility to 64 Freedom)

When shadows within are denied, your soul cannot acknowledge that you are being driven by desires rather than having the ability to respond to life freely. Use your awareness to delve deep into your soul. This will reveal to your consciousness insights on the polarities within you. With this newfound clarity reason will shine with brilliance thus illuminating the shadows of your soul. You will begin to experience freedom and creativity. Freedom to respond to life, not escape from it. Through voluntary creativity you can begin to construct the New Earth culture. The desire to give your all to the whole of life will be fulfilled in the freedom to respond.

128 Embracing Eternity:
(1 Eternity to 128 Compassion)

Aligning with the eternal, you are one with the source of all universes, the ever present wellspring that nourishes and sustains all worlds. When you journey the innumerable pathways of life, this eternal wellspring becomes the transmuting power of compassion. Allow compassion to permeate the essence of your being and you will be able to transmute the poisons of the world into the medicine that will rejuvenate the earth. Thus the healing waters of compassion will flow freely from the eternal wellspring of life.

129 Joyous Responsibility:
(22 Desire to 107 Responsibility)

Desire is the necessary urge that allows spirit to manifest as form. Yet desire also can create separation between you, as subject, and the other, as object. Perceiving others as objects is bound to be frustrating and will lead to hurt and anger. It is impossible to possess what you desire. Desire aligned with love can act as a guide to the manifestation of your survival and existence. When desire separates from love your desires become addictions. This is because you grasp for results rather than remaining one with the source. The ability to respond freely to life is found in the acknowledgment of the power of desire and yet remaining detached in regards to results. Turn desire into responsibility and travel a lighter, wider more joyous path.